A GIRL'S CRY IN THE DARK

Pain Is Just A 4-Letter Word

CHANTAY HARRIS

CHANTAY HARRIS

A Girl's Cry in the Dark

Contact the Author:
Email: teensexperiencelearninglife@yahoo.com

A GIRL'S CRY IN THE DARK

WHY THIS BOOK?

This book is no ordinary with thrills, special characters, twists, and turns. It is not about what to do and how to do it, whatever your "it" may be. Please keep in mind that this book is about pain, turmoil, confusion, torture, cries, hate, negativity, suicide, rape, dreams, visions, false hope, and changes. It may not be suitable for people who have such a wonderful life and born with the "silver spoon" in their mouths and cannot identify with the real struggle with identity or are infected by their negative household and communities.

I did not write this book to gather pity from readers. It is meant to build hope in all that is negative in your life as an adult and young adult. To learn to live today for a better tomorrow through the knowledge of knowing that life is real and there are consequences to every action we choose and every road we take in life.

This book is written most of all for me…. For closure, for healing.

Why "A Girl's Cry in The Dark? Because for over forty years of my life, I have experienced the pain of keeping all this bottled up inside my mind, heart, and soul. The embarrassment of my childhood, hate, pain, heartbreak, and anger; it's my time to release and exhale. I finally found joy today because I can speak to teen girls as a Mentor. My only heart desire is to make an active, positive difference in this world, our communities, and globally if possible. My story does not give a name to any of the characters; they are fully protected from any harm. Some are dead and gone. The acts that connected us are all forgiven because I forgive them too.

I wanted to share my story with everyone. It will help the following groups of people:

- The homeless women and girls who are victims of domestic violence.
- Those who have issues with being bullied.
- The teens who had to experience abortion, rape, or domestic violence.
- Those who experienced or are experiencing depression.
- Mothers who are unaware of the negative impact they pose on their daughters.
- Sex addicts.
- Failed relationships.
- Those who experience abandonment by their mothers and fathers.
- Awareness of spirituality.
- Mothers and fathers who mourn the loss of their children.
- Those interested in learning to love.

I am not sure if this book will touch your heart or give you enough conviction to ask for forgiveness from yourself and others who partake of your struggles. I only wish that it will provide you with a clear understanding of the choices we make at the beginning of life that will affect us throughout our lives. I can only pray that it will give you the sense to know that Spirituality is real. Please remember that you are important to this universe and that Pain is just a 4-letter word. Change will and can come for you, too, as it has for me for the betterment of my entire life and life purpose.

May this book be a blessing to each one of you.

TABLE OF CONTENTS

ACKNOWLEDGMENT

To every woman who supported this project, thank you once again for your continuous encouragement to continue going after my dream of being an Author.

Writing this book was an extraordinary journey from start to finish. Reliving the trials and tribulations that have contributed to my success in life has taught me that you can do much more than you think, no matter what life experiences that come your way. This story would not have even been possible without the spiritual guidance of my spirit and my ancestor's protection that allowed all the tests in my life. I truly appreciate each person who is familiar with my story and did not judge me for being who I am today.

I am especially indebted to my family, friends, and past relationships. Thank you all for the life experiences that were not all pleasurable but were lessons. This book is not meant to intentionally hurt anyone in any way or defame anyone in any way. It is my experience and expresses how I felt while going through each experience and having to relive it to complete this book. This book took me three years to complete due to the trauma that had to be recalled.

Most importantly, I am eternally grateful to the Most High and my Spirit Guide, who inspires and strengthens me to proceed with loving myself first and foremost. I am forever grateful for today; I am free, powerful, universally sound, and grounded in all positive energy.

Thank you all for purchasing a copy of my book.

DEDICATION

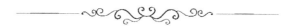

I dedicate this book to my parents, one of who has gone to her next life, the late Rosetta Allgood, who had a huge influence in and on my life. I also dedicate this book to my birth father, who I have never met according to my birth certificate, a huge secret no one spoke about. But the Universe has a way of revelation, which makes this book a matter of whose child is she?

I forgive you both.

I also dedicate this book to teen girls all over the world who have experienced things they could not speak about; maybe their voices will be heard after reading my book. I thank the Universe, The Most High, and Goddess MAAT for speaking and freeing me from the bondage of my mind. For once in my life, I am listening.

A BLACK WOMAN'S SUICIDE NOTE

I cannot take much more pain…
Of misunderstood emotions and strain.
Nor do I feel that no one hears
The voices in my head that cause my tears,
I'm tired of being so sad and blue…
Whatever happened to love so true?
Mom…, oh Dad, where are you now...
When my heart has been thrown all around?
You were supposed to protect me from this….
The knives, the drugs, rape, death of my children, and the
fists.
Oh, Why? Lord, must it be me?
What do I do, Lord? Where is the Key?
He hit me, raped me, and stole my soul.
Now I die inside, and no one knows.
Why can't anyone hear my cry?
I know if I kill myself, I will die.
Not ever feeling the happiness and joy of love
From anyone here or above.
Lord, guide your angels to protect me through the night,
And give me the answers as I sleep to escape this fright.

Written by: Chantay Harris

CHAPTER 1

MY TEEN CHALLENGE

I knew that my perky body was changing. How? Because the boys in my school would say things to me like, "Look at bubble butt." I was offended by their comments and torture. They would hit me in the butt whenever I bent over to drink out of the water fountain at our middle school. In the past, I would run after them to hit them back in frustration, but I could not catch them. I even got unwanted attention from older men with my tiny waist and round bottom at that time. I stayed active, which helped me to stay in shape. I was on the drill team in our community and modeled also. You might say I had a lot of curves in all the right places. I was in excellent shape. But it was a shame to say that my body was much like the home we lived in nice and attractive on the outside but messed up on the inside. But only a few knew the secrets, lies, and infidelity that went on. It was not a very happy place for me, and this is where I will start my story. Only negative comments from my mother about how "ugly" and "fat" I was. I never knew why that was my normal greeting from her all through my life until the day she died, including that Tuesday night before she passed away on Wednesday. No one paid any attention in our

5

home, just homework, eat, study, then bed; at a certain time, then the fighting, hitting, and arguing would start again between my mother and her partner. This drove me to appreciate all the attention I received outside my home at age fourteen.

Age 15

Well, I was fifteen and had a boy who was not from our town who liked me. We would ride his bike to my house and hang out front with our neighborhood friends. We were going steady. Meaning steady kissing, hugging, and touching, and it all felt good. I finally had someone who was really interested in me enough to tell me just how beautiful I was then. I started to dress up and do my hair to look older because he was a year older than me. He always teased me about my bedtime and having to go home at a certain time after school. Well, one night, I felt that I had been teased enough. I went to a "basement" party at a friend's home. Every adult can identify and know what happened at the basement parties; it was my first basement party. The party consisted of the green or red-light bulb in a light fixture with no cover, slow music from the albums played on a record player, vinyl records, of course. Boys came to the parties with one specific thing in mind: to grind on the girls and reach a creamy feeling between their legs. The girls would come dressed mostly in dresses or short skirts or skintight pants, spandex so that the hands of the boys would go easily up or down the outer parts of the clothing.

I arrived with one of my sisters, cousin, and friends. The boys were going crazy when we arrived. I had taken a drink from my mother's bar before I left for the party; I tiptoed behind the bar and took my first drink of vodka. It was not good tasting, I thought, but it was not so bad. I filled the bottle with water to replace what I drank so my mother and her partner would not know. I dressed seductively and went to the party with a little buzz in my head. I felt that nothing could go wrong tonight. Tonight was the night, and I knew my boyfriend would be there. I was looking hot and feeling sexy from head to toe. I was still a virgin. We arrived at the party, and it was filled with smoke. Some teens were smoking cigarettes, and some were smoking weed. I had never smoked before, and my boyfriend did not smoke either. He was a wrestler at the time in his high school. He did not do drugs or alcohol. He encouraged me not to do the same, so I did not. However, I did have the drink before the party, so I had the "buzz" I needed anyway. I was sexy and could get any boy I wanted at that time. So, I did.

My First Time

My boyfriend whispered things in my ear all night. Things that I had never heard any boy say to me before. He said he wanted to "stick his tongue in my mouth" and then did so. He was so handsome and very smooth with everything that he did and said. He kissed me. That was my first French kiss. His tongue filled my mouth, and his lips touched mine. All I could do was melt with the warm liquid flowing from his mouth to mine. The kiss was so wet and wonderful. His mouth stayed wet and moist each time he kissed me. His lips were full, and my lips would now stay wet and full of moisture, ready for the next kiss. It felt like we kissed for hours. My breast started to fill with anticipation, and I loved how I felt, although clueless. Later that evening, I became an expert at French kissing in the heat of the moment. His hands became smoother to the touch of my body. Now without me noticing because we had not stopped kissing this entire time, I completely forgot where we were. We had moved from the party room with the blue light to another room in another part of the house. It was the kitchen; it was dimly lit, and while moving, we were still kissing. But this was only the beginning. He lifted my small short tee shirt. It was sheer white and cotton. My nipples were so hard they showed through the shirt's front. It was wonderful! By this time, he had unhooked my bra.

However, it was now off and onto the floor. But my tee shirt was still on. How did he do that? I thought. When did that happen? My head was swimming so fast. So many thoughts ran through my mind mostly because of the alcohol. Thoughts like, what am I doing? Why does this feel so dam good? How far am I willing to go? Should I have sex or not? Would he get mad if I stopped him now? What will I do if he gets mad? Will he break up with me? I loved his hands all over my body. This is my boyfriend, and he told me he loved me, so I can give him what he wants to show my love to him. Then I was lost in ecstasy....

He led me by the hand to the upstairs bedroom. My heart was racing now. I was now in this moment, thinking this was going too far. I am a VIRGIN. I do not know how to do this! My head was screaming, "STOP NOW, TURN BACK, and YOU DO NOT HAVE TO DO THIS!!!" all at once, but my body wanted more.

I kept going up the stairs very afraid but said nothing to him. My other thoughts were that if he said he loved me, it should be ok, it will not hurt, he loves me, he will not hurt me.

He knew I was a virgin, so he may not want to go through with it. We will just lay and kiss on the bed.

We were now upstairs in the small bedroom to the right of the hall. It was very dark in the room, but there was a shade up, and we could see the full moonlight showing through the bedroom window as we entered the room. The moonlight was shining on the bed. My boyfriend, who loves me, whispered yet again that he "loved me," which he has told me for the past eight months of our relationship. It was a long eight months; we saw each other every day. Now we were in love; nothing could go wrong. My mother approved of him; it was perfect. He began kissing me with his moist tongue, and the moisture from my lips and between my legs was now at its highest peak.

"I am not ready to go any further," I said. He replied, "I thought you loved me." I told him that I did, but by this time, I began to shake for some reason every now and then. My body started to shake. I did not cause this at all. It did it on its own. He noticed and asked, "Are you scared?" I said, "Yes." He said, "I love you and will not hurt you at all," then started kissing me in the mouth and would not stop this time. In the heat of the moment, he had my tee shirt off. I felt the coolness of the room hit my body. The moonlight was hitting my body in such a way it made it look beautiful not only to my boyfriend but to me. This was the first time I had ever looked at my body under the moonlight in a mirror before. He said to me, "You are beautiful." My firm stomach was tight, my abs were very hard, and my waist was very small. I did look beautiful. This was his first time seeing my body without a shirt on. My smooth brown skin looked like cinnamon smoothed over a moist brown cake.

Well, I was mesmerized looking into the mirror at myself. Beauty and love filled my head for the very first time.

Now I was ready, or so I thought, but my body was speaking another language; it was still shaking now and then. He laid me down on the bed. By this time, he had taken off his shirt. His body was muscular, and he was very athletic. His body was brown-skinned, long, and very hard. The moonlight made him appear to be smooth and dreamy at the same time. He was so strong and looked like Super Man to me. The muscles were endless. I had no choice but to reach up for him as he stood before me. I sat up and felt every muscle I could above his waist. His body was tight, warm, and endlessly smooth. He turned around in front of me to see his back side. He had a perfect "V." His waist was small, his abs were a definite six-pack, and his skin was smooth. But the back side was even more appealing; his bottom was round and firm. Yes, I felt it, although he had not yet removed his pants. He turned back around to the front and got down on his knees. My body again started to shake. I did not understand why.

Was I this afraid? Then, as my body began to shake, he began to kiss me endlessly again. His smooth chest was now closer to mine, and my nipples were rubbing his skin now completely hard. This was the first time I felt a man's naked body. It was wonderful under my fingers.

What could possibly go wrong with this night? My body continued to shake out of fear of being completely naked. I felt a little ashamed for some reason, but I had gone too far now to think of turning back. He went on and on in a whisper, saying how beautiful my body was and that he had never seen any other body like this. He was now running his hands up my thighs and kissing my thighs. My body began to shake more and more now that it became uncontrollable. My teeth were shattering, and I could not stop them. My boyfriend noticed this happening. He stood before me and asked me if I was ok. I said, "Yes, but I don't know why my body is shaking so much." He began kissing me, and it would stop, and then I would be lost in his wet mouth. He had his hands all over my body now. I was not sure what was going on. The time seemed to stand still. He removed his blue striped boxer shorts, and I could see his manhood standing straight up. He knew he had to hurry because my body shakes were uncontrollable. The kiss made me calm down. But now, that did not work. Then I started shaking again. Oh well, anyway, he began to make motions between my legs. I had never felt this feeling before and will never forget it. He was experienced way more than I was.

None of my girlfriends who were having sex ever told me about a boy doing this. Oh yeah, they mentioned everything else he would do but not this! Well, I felt confused. Maybe he should not be doing this since they did not mention it at all. He was now between my shaking thighs. He tried to help me relax by rubbing his warm hands on my thighs and the back of my naked ass as I lay on my back on the bed. I can still see the moonlight. My body continued to shake. He tried to open my legs, but they would not budge. Finally, he stopped and then came back up to kiss me. My hidden area was filled with moisture and all kinds of first feelings. Again, he lay on top of me, kissing me, and his manhood was so hard he tried to open my legs, and they would not budge. They were locked so tight from the shakes that I could not open them either. So, he started filling my mouth with his wet tongue, then started to relax his manhood so that he could enter my body. It worked.

He relaxed, then moved his manhood which was now semi-hard and started to rub it against my warm moist patch of hair. My body still shook; however, it did feel good. It was my first time feeling good at this moment in time. My body started to respond to his rubbing. I finally relaxed under his touch again. He kissed and rubbed, and it felt good. I could handle this. My body jumped again from his touch in this private area. The time was endless. My body twitched and moved, it was inhumanly wet, I thought. He moved up and back on top of me. He rubbed his fingers between my legs, and my body responded in the moonlight. Moving back and forth, my legs relaxed and began to open wide. I still shook but not uncontrollably from fear, but this was another type of shake. This was my first time reaching orgasm with a boy; it was wonderful. I was in ecstasy.

My mind said stop here, but my body was screaming out for more. He then entered my body. It hurt so much that I screamed out. He was too excited and did not remember that this was my first time.

My body froze and I could not feel anything but pain! I wanted him to stop and get off, but he was in the moment and could not stop himself. It hurt so bad all I could feel was his large manhood going in and out of my body. It was painful. So, this is what the first time feels like, were my thoughts. The moments of pleasure were all gone. I never wanted to do this again! He tried to kiss me during the act and to get me to move as I had before this point, but my body was now rejecting his actions. Why now? I thought. But I just laid there and suffered in pain. My body rejected his kisses as well. Now they felt dry, hard, and again endless. He was excited, but I was not anymore. He finally reached his point of no return. We did not use a condom, nor did we use any clear understanding before we entered this zone. Now it was in the past. He finished. I was full of blood between my legs. I got up, ran to the bathroom with my clothes, and never returned to that house again.

CHAPTER 2

THE BREAKUP

Days and weeks went by. I had not seen nor heard from my boyfriend. He had another girlfriend who lived in the neighborhood, and she had more experience than I did. However, I had to go on with this secret of having sex in my head. My thoughts were, wow, and this is love? At that point, I knew I did not know what love really was. I did not see nor hear any signs of love at home. Now, I did not see or hear it on the streets or even with my boyfriend. About a month later, I saw him after a school basketball game. He came over to me and apologized for that night and said he was "now seeing another girl." I was heartbroken by how he told me and when he told me. I could not show pain because I was with my friends, and he was with his. So, I had to hide my true feelings. I wanted to run far away and cry. I knew I had no one to talk to about this because my first time was a secret, so I thought.

Well, one of his friends started to show me attention. I was a little leery at first, but he once told me that he thought I was beautiful and that he was "watching me with his friend." He said he did not think I "would have sex with him." I felt so stupid, and that is what I called myself, "STUPID." I hated myself now because if he knew how many of his other friends knew. So, I ignored my thoughts and became his friend for vengeance. I figured it was his friend; why not? I had nothing to lose. Not knowing this new friend's intentions, I did not care at the time.

So, he came around to see me, and I would catch the bus to his home to see him. My new friend and I became very close. He had a mother, father, and siblings. He was tall and very handsome. I fell instantly in love with him. He worked and had his own car, and his family had a beautiful and loving home. They showed me love and acceptance. A few months passed, and then we were in his home alone for the first time. He was a handsome young man, and his height and smile were what attracted me to him the most. His body was firm and strong, and I loved his country look. He was popular like his friend, my ex.

We were alone in the house and went to his room. He kissed me, and it felt like chocolate bites on a warm day. Melting on my mouth were his warm, full wide lips, and his tongue felt like chocolate melting and going down sweet. I was instantly hot all over, although I had not been touched like the first time. This time is much nicer. His hands were warmer, softer, and gentler. We removed our clothes; we did not know how much time we had before his parents returned home. He looked at my beautiful fit body, small waist, and round, smooth, soft ass and went into shock. I kept it tight for a reason, and this may be my ticket, I thought, to get what I wanted from a man. I loved my body, and I kept it in top shape. He removed his clothing, and his body was so strong, tall, lean, and brown. He was a beautiful chunk of a man, were my thoughts. We lay on the bed, and love filled the air, and the scent of a woman's moisture and a man's odor ripped through our noses. Our bodies felt perfect together. He was very gentle and slow in movement; nothing was forced. "What happened to the shakes?" I asked myself. Anyway, he moved his lips from my nipples to my navel. My thought was, here we go again. But this time was different; it was like ecstasy with a cherry on top of the chocolate. I was savoring the moment and relaxing through his touches. He then got on top of me.

Now we lay on the bed. We rubbed our private parts. My body was hot. The way he moved his hands felt like warm butter moving throughout my skin and body. He touched me in all the right ways. I lost control and allowed him to enter me. This was the first time a breakup felt so good. I was so lost in this young man that I never even thought of my ex-boyfriend again. I was in love.

CHAPTER 3

THE PREGNANCY

WEll, my new boyfriend and I were inseparable. However, he was seeing another girl, but I did not care. He told me he loved me, and that was all I saw. He would pick me up, take me places, spend money on me, and we would go to movies and have so much sex in the backseat of his car. It was wonderful until….

I missed my period

My mother was a woman who thought about the finer things in life. But her children, at times, I guess, like any other children, were in her way. She had five from our father, her husband, and the last one from her lover of many years. She was not happy at all with any of the men she had flings with over the years. But this book is not about that. I missed my period and had to inform her of that. When I did so, she took me to the community doctor. Everyone in our town went to this doctor. So, when she took me there, everyone we knew was there, which means the people older than me. The nurse called my name and gave me a cup to pee in. What do I know? I was Fifteen AND PREGNANT!

Not a good sign or a good way to start this day. I don't have to tell you how upset my mother was with me. I was now a "whore," "bitch," and every other name you could have thought of as an angry mother. She said that I had to get an abortion, and that was final. She told me that "I am not bringing any babies in her house to raise," which she said repeatedly. I was in shock. My thoughts were, how could I be pregnant? I only did it twice! I was equally upset. Anyway, the drive home was about ten minutes, but with her yelling, cursing, and calling me names, it seemed like five hours. We arrived home, and she told the whole family, my sisters, brothers, and her lover, that I was pregnant and a whore. I was truly the black sheep of the family anyway. That will be explained in another chapter.

The following day, she contacted a doctor at the hospital pavilion in the town where my boyfriend lived. She made the appointment. That following Monday, she took me there. She was upset because she had to go to work by 3 pm and my appointment was at 1 pm. She cursed me again all the way to the appointment in the car. As I sat there, all I could think about was what I would do now. I did not know, but I knew that I better not say a word. I did not know what an abortion was, let alone how to endure it. I had no clue what to expect. I was in a daze like a dream for the entire ride. She talked, yelled, and told me how much of an embarrassment I was to her all the time and now even more. She told me that I was a disgrace to the family. I sat alone and scared.

We arrived at the abortion clinic. She parked the car. I got out; she was screaming by this time. I stayed quiet and terrified, and my body and teeth began to shake violently again. I remember this feeling; it won't go away and I could not control it. We went into the building and stood at the tall desk where the nurses placed a sign that read "Receptionist." The welcome nurse asked us to "sign in." My mother signed her name and my name, and we sat down. I sat quietly; she said nothing. I could tell by how her leg moved back and forth as she crossed them in her sitting position and then uncrossed them that she was visibly upset.

The nurse called my name. My mother mentioned again that she had to leave and go to work. I said nothing. My thoughts were, do not leave me here alone, please. But I would not speak that from my mouth. I dare not. She would have punched me. I have been there and did not have to be reminded how much it hurt. The nurse led me into an exam room. It had a table with those stirrups, sink, cabinets, and tile floor and was very clean. The nurse asked me some personal questions regarding my period, to which I responded. I wanted to tell her how scared I was, but my mother was sitting there. I dare not speak out of turn. Plus, the nurse was an older white lady. Her face was stern. She did not crack a smile at all the entire time we were greeted and taken back to the cold exam room. It was August, so we welcomed the cool room and the air conditioning. She gave me the usual cup and asked me to pee in it. I left to do so and then returned to the room. Once I entered the room, the nurse and my mother immediately stopped talking. I knew the conversation was about me, of course. I stood until she directed me to what to do next. She told me to remove my clothes, put on the paper dressing over my body opening in the front, and then lay on the table. My mother left the room. I figured she would wait for me in the waiting room. I did as instructed by the nurse. I undressed and put on the paper cape, opening in the front. Then I lay on the table. It seemed like an eternity until the doctor arrived. It was now very cold, and I was shaking so badly, but I could not control it. My thoughts were, I wonder what he is going to do. This thought just screamed and screamed in my head. I began to tear up, but the tears would not fall.

The doctor came in. He was a short round white man with a bald head on top and hair on the sides. He did not smile or greet me at all. The nurse was with him. I sat up on the table. He looked over the chart the nurse had given to him. He told me that I was pregnant. I knew that but said nothing. I looked at him very afraid because he was cold and not compassionate. He never made eye contact at this point. I watched him. He went to the sink, washed his hands, dried them, and put on gloves. He told me to lie down. I did so. He told me to open my gown in front. I did so. He felt on my firm breast. He felt on my flat stomach, and then he tried to open my legs. My body was shaking so badly that my teeth began to shatter also uncontrollably. I was embarrassed and wondered what this was about and what was wrong with me. I was so afraid I was out of control at this point.

The doctor got angry as he tried hard to force my legs apart. His face turned red. The nurse, who was still in the room watching, came over to me on my right as I lay on the table. She told me to relax. She began rubbing my arm. Her hands were warm through the plastic latex gloves. My body began to relax under her low voice, repeating herself as she tried to get me to relax. She, as a woman, had to know how scared I was, I thought to myself. I just wanted to leave, but I knew my mother and her wrath was much worst at this moment; I dare not. I lay trying hard to relax. Time just went by. He placed my feet on the hard circle things at the end of the table, but my knees kept touching. The nurse rubbed my legs until I stopped shaking and then lowered my knees. Finally, it appeared that my body was now a little less tensed up. The doctor sternly told me to move down closer to the end of the table. I did so inch by inch. Not sure what will happen next. He told me, "More, more, more." When I was at the end of the table, I did not notice that my knees were locked again. He grew angry and pulled on my knees so hard I thought he would have broken them. Where was my mom while he was doing this to me? That hurt, but I said nothing as usual, just laid there on the hard table. He touched my middle part with the tip of his finger. I thought I would jump off the table. I did not want him touching me in my private area, were my thoughts. Those thoughts were very loud at this point. I hated him! The nurse asked me to relax and told me that he was only going to examine me on the inside. This was the first time I had ever experienced this type of activity with any doctor. The Primary Care Doctor would only check my ears, heart, eyes, and mouth, and that was it.

I made it through that rough ordeal. He stuck not only one but three fingers inside of me, pressed on my stomach very hard, then moved his fingers around more and went deeper with those fingers. He took out his fingers and told me to sit back and sit up. I did so. I watched him. I was in pain now. I sat up and looked at him, but still no eye contact. After this invasion, he could at least look at me. He had a stern and cold look, as did the nurse. He assured me again that I was pregnant and had to come back for two more days to complete the procedure. He told me that the nurse would call my mother to inform her of the "cost of the abortion." The doctor told me to get dressed and that he would give me a few pills to take tonight before I left. The doctor and nurse both left the room. I was alone in the cold, clean room, still sitting on the bed; I cried. I mean, I cried and cried. My thoughts were that my mother was going to kill me! Then I thought about what an abortion is and how I could get out of this! I cried uncontrollably for about ten minutes, and the nurse returned to the room. She told me to get dressed, and then she left again. She saw that I was physically upset but said nothing to assure me that things would be ok. She was almost like a robot, I thought at the time. I wiped my face, slowly moved from the table, and began getting dressed. I placed the paper dressing in the silver container with the black lid and left the room feeling lost and alone. I just knew my mother was waiting for me. I returned to the desk and asked the nurse sitting there if my mother was there. She said, "No, she left long ago." I was in shock.

I stood still for a moment and could not feel my legs. I had no money and no ride. I asked the nurse if I could call home. She dialed the number, and my sister answered. I asked if mom was there. She told me that mom said I should walk home. I told her I could not walk home because it was a half-hour drive. It would take me forever. She hung up on me. She was always mean; she and I were always fighting. I hung up the phone on my end. The nurse at the desk took the receiver and placed it back on the phone. I stood still, thinking about who I could call. I then said grandpa to myself. I asked the nurse to dial another number. My grandma answered. She and grandpa were always there for me, no matter what. And I loved them so much. They showed me so much love that I would be full of their love coming and going.

My grandparent picked me up as always. They pulled up, and my grandpa got out of the driver's side of his Lincoln and came to open the back-passenger side door for me. I got into the car. This was the best thing that has happened to me in a few days. The black leather seats felt so nice, and being with them, I felt safe. My grandma asked what I was doing all the way out there at the hospital office. I told her, "I had to see the doctor," and that was it. She asked how I got there. I said, "Mom." My grandpa asked if I was ok. I said yes and sat quietly. I was too embarrassed and had humiliated my mom enough to tell them why I was there. They asked no more questions. We drove home in silence. My grandpa never played the radio in his car. They were the best grandparents in the world to me. They dropped me off at my front door, and my grandfather got out to open my door. I hugged and kissed my grandparents and thanked them both. They drove off.

CHAPTER 4

THE ABORTION

I arrived home, and my mother had already left for work. I was relieved she was not there to express more anger. When she returned home tonight, I would be in bed. She usually got home around 12 am. I went into the house and started my homework, then housework as we had to do daily.

Some of my siblings were doing their homework; others were watching TV. A quiet night, I thought. The next day, my mother told me to get up, get dressed, and go back to the doctor. I had forgotten that I had to go back. I did as told. Again, she cursed me all the way in the car and told me how disappointed she was and how I was an embarrassment to her. No one knew about the abortion but my brothers, sisters, and her partner. I said nothing, of course.

We arrived.

So many thoughts were going through my mind. Why could I not just stand up for myself and let her know I am scared and afraid of being left alone with this doctor? We arrived at the building. She parked and we both got out. She walked before me quickly into the building. We both signed in as usual, and I sat down. My mother was still standing at the receptionist's desk and gave the nurse some cash. I was not sure at that time how much it was for this abortion, but I found out later the cost was two hundred and fifty dollars. I just thought that here we go again; this time, this is it. Or so I thought. She paid the nurse and left. I sat in the waiting room alone. I figured she was coming back. There was no way she would just leave me again in this place. She never returned. The cold, stern-looking nurse yet again called my name. I got up and followed her through the door and into the same room as before. The room looked the same. It was cold, dry, clean, and lonely. No thrills, pictures, books, nothing on the walls.

She told me to disrobe. I did not understand why I had to keep taking all my clothes off each time. But as always, I did as I was told, challenging no one and asking no questions. I was in the same position as the previous day. I sat alone quietly. The nurse came in and out. I just stared in a daze, not thinking anything or looking at anything or anyone. Just dazed into thin air, then the doctor came into the room—the same short, balding round white man with his clean white lab coat. Again, no eye contact. He told me what to do. I did it as instructed. Lie down, I did; sit up, I did; roll over, I did. He then told me to move closer to the edge of the bed as he had done the day before. Of course, my knees locked up and were shaking violently. I was not prepared for what he would say to me next. I guess he had it with me with the legs locking and not relaxing. He then said to me, "Open your legs, you little nigger." I was in shock. What did he just say? Maybe I was so afraid that I was now hearing things. He then said, "I am going to make sure you don't have a nigger babies, you whore. Open your fucking legs, you whore". Then he yanked my legs so hard I thought he ripped them off. He then stuck his three fingers in my womanhood so hard I nearly jumped from the table; no moisture, no ready, set, go, this time. He was pissed. He moved them around so hard and fast, then yanked his fingers out of me and told me, "Sit up, you nigger." I was a lap dog, now a slave, I thought, and truly, this is a violation of my girlhood also, I knew that. He told me to sit up and get dressed. He and the nurse left the room. I was left alone, violated, humiliated, and now a nigger!

I could not wait to get out of this room and tell my mom. She would curse him out, I am sure of that! I got dressed in a hurry after I gained my composure. I left the room to find that my mom was not there. The cold nurse followed me to the desk and told me to return to the room. I followed her, sat back on the bed as instructed, and the doctor came back in. I guess he was not finished humiliating me. He probed me here and there and felt me up as he did before. I was his lap dog and his slave, I thought at this point. He knew I was alone, fifteen, and clueless. Anyway, he told me to take this syrup-tasting liquid. I did, not sure what it was, but I was his lap dog, so it was what I was told to do. Listen to your elders is what we were taught. Don't ask any questions; shut up. It was all that I knew, and I am now doing just that. Let this tiny white man violate you and shut your black mouth, little girl. I did just that.

This was my entire fault. I thought my rights got taken away from me when I had sex the first time. But I must have asked for this. I am being punished as my mother would say, "You get what you deserve;" "you made your bed, you lie in it." She spoke these words to me over and over throughout this whole ordeal, almost like she knew what would come next, I thought. Ok, I said to myself. The nurse returned and gave me three little white pills and a small paper cup full of water. The water was nice and cold. I put the pills in my mouth and then drank the water to get them down. She left the room, and I was left alone staring at the devil's face. He did not make eye contact; I was looking right at him, upset. He told me the pills I took would start the abortion process and that I had to come back tomorrow for the procedure. The doctor told me that I could not change my mind. If I wanted to now, the baby would be born deformed. "This is it," he said and then left the room. I was so upset I sat on the table and cried.

Finally, I dried my tears, wiped my face, got off the table, and went to the waiting room. My mother was not there. Again, I called my grandpa and grandma, who picked me up and took me home. By this time, I figured they knew what I was doing at the doctor's office two days in a row, knowing that my mother had dropped me off and I was supposed to be walking home, not riding along with them. My mother was pissed when she found out I called them to pick me up and bring me home. I forgot to mention her choice of words for me when she found out. You can probably figure out what those words were at this point. I was a whore, nigger, good for nothing, an embarrassment to the family, a disgrace, and most of all, a bitch. Been there, done that, and received these were the new names that everyone had for me but my grandparents. They told me that they love me and JESUS loves me - so do I - which is what my grandparents always told me.

When my grandpa pulled up to my house, I burst into tears. I was so upset. My grandma asked me what was wrong with her calm low-pitched voice. My grandpa turned around and looked at me and knew something was wrong. I was so upset I could only get out a little, and they could not understand my gibberish. My grandma told me to calm down so they could understand me. I calmed down through the tears and said the doctor called me a "nigger and a whore." She said in a concerned voice, "Why did he say that to you?" I said because my mother made me go to him for an abortion. They were both very surprised because they were silent at first. Then my grandma reached for me from the back seat, and I reached over the front seat to hug her, and my grandpa had his hand rubbing my back. I was crying so hard. She told me that I will be ok that JESUS loves me. I did not know why she always said that to me growing up, but she did. I paid it no mind. I did not know who JESUS was at this time because we were Jehovah's Witnesses growing up. That was where our mother took us. We all slept through the teachings at the Kingdom Hall. I cried in my grandmother's arms. I wiped my face and dried my tears. My grandpa came around the passenger rear door to let me out of the car. He gave me a big hug and I felt safe with them; they really cared for me. I knew that. I hugged grandma and kissed her through the car passenger side window. She assured me that everything would be ok. I went into the house.

My mother left me a note to wait up for her. I was now scared. I got the note and waited up as instructed. I sat at the table doing my homework when she came in. Some before that point, I had spoken to my boyfriend. I finally told him that I was pregnant; he did not know. He did not make much of an expression via phone. I told him that my mother was making me get an abortion. He was silent on the phone. I also told him what happened to me at the doctor's office over the last two days and told him everything the doctor did and said to me. He told me that he would call me right back. About an hour before my mother came home, my boyfriend's parents called me on the phone and made me tell them the story of the pregnancy and about my experience at the doctor's office as well as the abortion process. I told them how scared I was, how upset my mother was at me, and how I was a disgrace to the family and her. They wanted to meet with my mother because they did not believe in abortions; they were Christians. I knew that.

My mother arrived at about 11:30 pm that night. I saw my mother getting angry at the sight of me. I figured she was mad at the doctor for what he said to me and that they told her before I did. Little did I know that was not why she was angry. We sat at the dining room table. My mother looked at me, and if looks could kill, I would have been dead right then and there. I looked away. My eyes were red, and my face was swollen from the mental torture that played through my mind. The doctor's visits and my new names were all too much for me. We sat quietly at the table. My mother asked me what happened at the doctor's office today. I told her what he said and what he did to me through tears. She listened for the first time. She looked at me in disgust. I looked away while wiping my tears. My boyfriend kept looking at me and I did not even make eye contact with him. He sat and said nothing. His father told my mother that he did not think that she should make me go back and have the abortion and that they would help me care for the baby. My mother responded, and they left. When they did, my mother cursed and yelled at me, "You are having the abortion. And there is no guarantee that this boy is going to be able to care for you and a baby." Those were her words. My mother was dead set against any of what they were saying and told me that it was "her final decision." I sat and cried. She told me to shut up and to stop crying. She told me she is the one that must deal with looking at me pregnant and that I am not bringing any babies into her home. "You got what you deserved," she said, "and I'm taking you back there tomorrow."

I was every name in the book and embarrassed her by calling me the names. I was called yet again "bitch," "ugly," "fat," and "sickening," and some other things all came from her mouth at the same time. She threatened, "You better not embarrass me ever again." She then punched me in the face. I was so upset all I could do was cry all night.

I got no sleep. I could not call my boyfriend at all that night. I was all alone and on punishment. I got dressed like the robot and lap dog I was and got into my mother's car the following day. I had an idea of what would happen next if I did not get into the car. We were silent on the ride to the doctor's office. It was like driving to hell, and this is what hell feels like. She was driving me to the devil himself, was the second thought.

We arrived. I got out of the car, and she pulled up front. She was not even going into his office with me to tell this guy off. I guessed not. The next thing I knew, she pulled off. I never felt so alone in my life. I went inside; something was telling me to just run away. But I had no place to go. If I went to my boyfriend's house, she would go there and pull me out by my hair; that was a fact. I just did as I had done the two days before. I went inside and signed in at the receptionist's desk. I was the only one in the waiting room. I sat and waited for my name to be called. But this time was different. I was waiting for an extra-long time for some reason or another. I sat, got up, and walked to the receptionist's desk to call my boyfriend. The nurse would not let me make a call for some reason today. Prior to that, it was not a problem. She told me, "No personal calls are to be made," and asked, "Did you see the sign?" I noticed the sign when she pointed to it on the right side of the window. I had not noticed the sign, and she never directed me to it before today. I quietly went back to my seat and sat down.

The devil's helper nurse called my name, and I followed her to the cold, clean room. She told me to undress and put on the paper cape, and the doctor would be in. I did as she instructed, "Yes, master," I spoke silently in my mind. I began to cry softly. I was so scared. The doctor came in and told me to lie on the table and move forward to the end of the table, where he sat between my legs, same as usual. He told me to open my legs. The nurse came in and draped a white sheet across my legs, and there was now a pad of some sort on the table also. He put another pad on the table under my ass and on the bottom of the table also. In the room was a machine of some sort with a hose at the end of it. The hose was clear, round and small, and short in length. The machine looked like a grey vacuum cleaner; it was on a stand, nothing I had seen before this day. As I lay back, the doctor instructed the nurse to put things on the small table beside a round, low stool. He washed his hands, put on gloves, then sat back down on the little round seat below him and moved closer to the table I was lying on. I did not know what he was going to do. The nurse came over to me and put a plastic tube-like thing over my nose and mouth. The doctor said nothing to me at all. The next thing I knew, I was getting dizzy and sleepy. But I was not sleeping. I just felt that way.

Nothing prepared me for what would happen next. The devil and his nursemaid did not tell me what would happen next. My evil mother did not prepare me for what would happen next. But I am preparing you all who have never had an abortion from a doctor from HELL BEFORE! The next thing I knew, I felt the doctor shove this hose-type thing into my girl hole and pushed it in so hard I jumped. He told me, "Lay still nigger." I was dizzy and had this thing over my face; the noise this thing made was a quiet buzzing sound when he turned on the machine.

I felt so uncomfortable. The hose was inside my body. The machine was turned on, and in an instant, I felt like my insides were being ripped apart from my body. I was in so much pain from the sucking action that was taking place that, in my mind, I was screaming and screaming. But I could not scream from my covered mouth. It was so painful that I passed out. This went on for what seemed like hours, although it was a short amount of time. I had passed out from the pain; it was something I would never forget. "You deserve this since you decided to have sex and get pregnant," was what I could hear my mother saying. But the pain was out of this world. I slept off the pain on the table. Before I knew it, I had awakened. The nurse was at my table on the right side this time. She was wiping up something from the floor. I saw her with a mop. I wondered what she was cleaning up since the place was spotless. She said nothing when she saw that I moved my head. My legs were down; the sheet was over me, clean and white. I was just lying there. I had no clue what happened. I just knew it was the worst pain I had ever felt at this point. She told me to get up slowly and to get dressed. I guess this was it. I thought it was over, and now my mother would no longer be mad at me. I can now be treated like a family member again. Or so I thought. I was in so much pain trying to sit up and use my stomach muscles. There was so much pain between my legs, and they had left blood all over the inner parts of my legs. It was a horrible scene under the lily-white sheet. The nurse gave me paper towels wet with water; they were warm. She gave me plenty to clean between my legs, private parts, inner thighs, and butt area.

She gave me some dry towels to dry myself off. I could barely open my legs at this point. I was so sore and embarrassed I pissed on myself, and that even was painful. Once dried, the nurse gave me a sanitary pad to put on. I slowly got off the table and got dressed. I was crying the entire time I put on each piece of clothing. I was disgusted with myself as my mother was with me. How could I be so stupid to have sex and now abortion and a disgrace to my family? I hated myself for the very first time. "I am now marked," I said with pain and disgust. These were my new names. I was very upset and mad, and this was like hell.

I left, called my boyfriend, and informed his parents about my ordeal, and they were in shock. All they could do was say, "I'm sorry." I was truly upset. My grandparents picked me up and I informed them as well. That was when I received the most beautiful package of love, hugs, and caring throughout this journey. They took me to dinner, but I had no appetite and just stared into space as they talked or tried to talk to me about my mother and how they did not understand why she would let me go thru such pain and torture. They had no answers, and neither did I. I just sat and stared, not wanting to be there or anywhere else. I arrived home and my mother whipped my ass well by punching me in the head, face, back, and arms. I endured pain on top of pain that day.

Of course, I recovered from the outer pain, but the pain and suffering from the abortion still haunt my mind. Every day, I was reminded by my mother that I was a disgrace, whore, and lazy. I was the only one of her children who cleaned the home and did all my chores. She knew that. Every day, she told me how ugly I was and how I would not amount to anything. That went on for months. I just walked around as a robot. One of my siblings and I fought all the time, and she started calling me embarrassing names. She was one who I started to hate all so very much through my teen years. She was meaner than me, but no one saw that because I was the one marked. She was the one who started the fights and said hateful things no one heard; they would only hear mine. Hate for myself and my sister and mother filled my mind.

I turned mean, very mean and bitter in all my actions.

CHAPTER 5

THE HEART KNOWS

The heart knows what I am feeling…
Although hidden so deep inside.

The pain is what causes my anger;
I guess I will hold onto it to protect the latter.

No wonder why I stand alone
In this world, on this day, my heart turned to stone.

Why do I have to warm so meek?
I am the victim of my own mind, thoughts I guess I will keep.

Why cannot I just stand up tall and strong in this hardness of
life?
Why don't I just speak up to end this strife?

The moistness of life in my heart is what I want to feel,
But instead, I just let those around me steal, steal, and steal.

Not knowing any joy but pain…
These negative things are more familiar, along with strain.

Can anyone see the thump of it?
Only the heart knows how it sits.

Written by Chantay Harris

35

CHAPTER 6

AFTER THOUGHT

Abortion, the dictionary reads. Induced termination of pregnancy before the fetus can survive. A fatally premature expulsion of a fetus from the womb. (According to Webster's II, New Riverside Dictionary).

Genesis 1:26, And God said, "Let us make man in our image, after our likeness: and let them have dominion over the fish, of the sea and over the fowl of air, and over the cattle and over the earth, and over every creeping thing that creepeth upon the earth." (KJV Hebrew-Greek Key Word Study Bible)

Jeremiah 1:5, "Before I formed thee in the belly I knew thee; and before thou camest forth out of the womb I sanctified thee, and I ordained thee a prophet unto the nations." (KJV Hebrew-Greek Word Study Bible)

Abortion is such a harsh word, but not as harsh as the procedure itself. At the time, I did not know the impact an abortion would have on me mentally and physically. No one prepared me for the procedure. I did not know the doctor's motivation, and I never expected him to say the things he said to me. I remember being mentally and physically abused during the three-day process by the doctor and, most of all, by my mother. I just knew she would protect me. No protection ever came. I remember being made to feel that I was too young to mother a child. Maybe at that time, I was. I thought that my mother knew more than I did with the struggles she had with many children in her life. I didn't know at that time that she was truly unhappy with being a mother.

Never did I realize in the years to come that the things that are done when an abortion is taking place would still impact my life today at age 50+. Since the abortion, I have not been able to have any children born alive. What else did the doctor do to me? Was it the doctor's fault? Read on; it gets better. I got pregnant three more times following that time in my life. It all got worse for me living in Hell every day of my life from that point on until now. I carried full term nine months. Read on, not regular births, just a bunch of funerals. Death was all around me every day, and I never knew.

Do I believe that the reasons for my children's untimely deaths resulted from the abortion? Yes, it played a huge part in the future of my life today. Do I think my mother was a contributor and conspirator to this act? Of course, I do.

If you are thinking of having an abortion because your mother is a hag, a person to make you feel less than a person, you are a slave to her thoughts, words, and actions. Think again. Or maybe you have had an abortion, perhaps more than one. I don't know if you had it back in the 70s or 80s or 90s or this century. Technology today makes it a lot easier. But the results and the mental anguish are the same. If you have a heart turned to stone, you know it will continue to affect your life today. I did not know that my mother's decision would affect me for the rest of my life. I told you about the physical side of it and about my past pregnancy. The following chapters will be a little more descriptive; I feel you need to know. Every mother needs to know. Maybe you are a mother who has had an abortion. Why would you want this for your child? Is it because you survived, or so it appears that you survived through it? Did you prepare your child for it before you made this decision for her? Don't do it, and do not make her go through with the abortion. Please. Maybe abortions are a part of your life and your family's life. For some, it is a form of birth control. For others, it is a way to hide from themselves and their responsibilities. My heart is saddened for you. I weep at your pain daily.

Too many young girls are forced to go through an abortion process. They are made to believe that this is a way out of the problem or pregnancy condition. But child, I am here to tell you that there are more meaningful ways to control whether you want to have children or not. I can only explain what it did to me and how I felt about it then and now.

Mentally, abortion no longer affects me today. I have learned after the recurring nightmares that would haunt my dreams time after time following that very day that I had to let it go; otherwise, the torture would not stop. I had to learn to forgive myself. Before that, for years, I awakened from a bad dream, thinking I was in the eye of the devil and its trolls. I was living a life that was a total lie. I was in complete darkness. Once I got older, I discovered what the process did to our bodies and the unborn child. There are reasons that you may feel abortion is the answer. You are 10-13 years of age, raped and incest happens, and you may feel abortion is the solution. I cannot speak to that. I can speak to the process, spiritually, mentally, and physically what it does to you. Some people are vessels just to get the child here. Every birth is a reason. We cannot choose our parents, trust me. If we could, I would have made better choices even at that age.

Just picture a living, breathing being created by The Most High figure on your table. Although still breathing, you may not see or hear the breathing. But in all, it still breathes. It has life. It has breath and all the cells of a living being created by God. Now the devil enters the room, and you are there in the room also. It is dark, but you are forced to be there to watch. You see something hover over your child, hit the living created gift from God, and crush the brain, the seed. That blunt object sucked the life from the once living being, and maybe there is blood splattered all over the table and your face while you just sat there saying nothing. But one thing is for sure; someone told you that you had a living created being God figure, a seed breathing there before this happened. You, the devil, and mother who knew were sure of that a baby. Then your living gift was swiped away while you watched. You felt the pain, you knew it was breathing, and you knew without a shadow of a doubt that this was your gift given to you by God the Creator. What do you do? What do you say? How do you stop it? You were forced to stand there and give up your gift beyond your control. Are you still held accountable for that life? Should you feel guilty? Will this destroy your life? Was it meant to? How do you feel as a mother who has had this done? What about those mothers who made this choice for their daughters to cover up something? Are they held accountable at the end of this lifetime, or will they receive their karma now? What are you really hiding? Do you go on with your life? Is the father who knew as well held accountable spiritually? If so, how?

What about your unborn child? Where do they really go? Did they have a choice? Why not? What form of birth control will you use next? Fathers, where are you, and what do you have to say about your daughters having an abortion? Don't they deserve life? You do.

Ponder over these questions; let's move on to Chapter 7.

CHAPTER 7

PREGNANCY # 2, #3 AND #4 - HELL WAS NOW MY HOME

Ages 16, 17, and 18, I was now living out every name my mother and others ever called me. I was the "whore," "the evil one," "fat," "ugly," "the bitch," "the meanest person on earth," and "school dropout," "the one who would amount to nothing," "nigger," "slut," "freak," and some. These were my names from the age of 15 through 18. After that age, the names got worst.

Again, I got pregnant by my boyfriend; his family was the only ones that accepted me. I was not accepted in school, at home, and in my community; his home was my peaceful place, and I needed them. I had turned to be so mean, and my behavior showed it; my posture showed it too. I had the biggest attitude at home and school. My school made my mother drop me out due to being a pregnant teen. Back then, you had to go to night school if you were a pregnant teen. Today, things are much different. But most of all, I hated

41

myself. I looked into the mirror every day, and all I could see was this ugly whore, as my mother called.

I was a disgrace, and I was disgusted with myself. I was living out the rest of the lies; they all became truth. That is what I did and how I walked. When my mother found out that I was pregnant, she was livid. I had never seen a woman so mean and did not think her wrath could get any worse. But it did. I am not painting her out to be this unloving mother; hate was love to me. That is all I knew. My siblings got treated ok, and they all have their own stories. But she was something else behind closed doors. No one else saw this in my mother. She was loved by many, and her children loved her too. I loved my mother and tried hard then and throughout my years to please her; I jumped when she said jump. This torture lasted all the way up until she died in 2002. I tried very hard, but this book is not about her and how mean she was. It is about revealing the hurt she caused and how the words she spoke molded who I became. She played a huge part in it, and I don't blame her. I have since forgiven her as well as myself.

Back to my story. Yes, pregnant again. She hated me even more. Of course, the cursing came at me left and right like blows to the mind, body, and soul. The separation between my siblings and me got worst. We grew further and further apart. My oldest sister, who was two years older than me, had dropped out of high school and moved in with her boyfriend, who did not even speak English. He came from Puerto Rico speaking Spanish. She was in love, and my mother did nothing to stop her from moving out as a teenager.

Once she found out that I was pregnant, things began to spiral downhill. I knew it would. However, I was not having an abortion this time, so we argued and fought. She repeatedly said I was not "bringing any babies into her house."

As my stomach grew, she hated me more. My sister caused so much more pain because she was mean. I was angry all the time. I hated this baby and hated life. But my boyfriend's parents bought me clothes as I grew, and I wore his shirts as I became heavier. They provided food when I was hungry. My mother did nothing for me throughout my pregnancy, as she said. I could not go on family outings to the beach or any place they went. I was made to stay at home. She took me out of school because I was an embarrassment. I was the only pregnant one in my grade at my school. I was called every name in the book at school. The teens were very cruel. I endured it all and kept up my grades. My boyfriend tried hard to make things better, but it was impossible. I hated life and him at this point. I was very bitter and angry and pushed him away every chance I got. He was a good young man. He tried hard, but my environment and I made things worse for me. It did not matter; he had other girls anyway. Plus, I was angry at myself. My mother gave me more negative words each time she saw how ugly and fat I grew. I gained sixty pounds, and it was not cute. She put me out of her house. I ran to my boyfriend's home.

They prayed for me and the pain I suffered. When my mother found out that I was living there, she forced me to come back home. I went as commanded. When I returned home, it was even more torture waiting for me.

Time went on. I was sad; with each day that went by, I was fat and miserable. One time I remember my brother throwing darts at my stomach, trying to hit my baby. He threw darts from the living room hallway to the bathroom each time I tried to pass by. He missed each time. I did nothing. "You get what is coming to you" is all I heard from my mother. I believed that with each day, I grew more and uglier to her and my family. I stayed inside because I was embarrassed.

My boyfriend's family threw me a baby shower. I had many gifts. I knew my mother would not be there, but that was ok. I was noticed and loved for a day. It was beautiful that his family really cared for me. I was happy for one day. I ate good food, had new clothes and baby clothes, pampered the whole day, and they ensured I had everything I needed and a crib for my home and their home. They had to spend hundreds of dollars. They were so happy for me and showed me so much love. They prepared their home for the baby. Once over, I took half the gifts home to my home. My mother forbade me from bringing any baby items into the home, so he had to take it all back to his house. I was upset. But there was nothing I could do about it. Time was coming soon for the baby to be born, and I knew I could not bring my baby home to this house. She was not going to let that happen. To this day, that is the best family I had ever met when it came to true unconditional love.

I went into labor after full nine months; it was now time. I was in so much pain and suffered long before I told anyone I was in labor. My water broke at home. My mother took me to the hospital and dropped me off at the emergency entrance. I went into the emergency room entrance and told the nurses I was in labor, which they could see. The nurse sat me in a wheelchair and wheeled me to a room. I did as she instructed, and the pain worsened. I cried out, but no one was there to tell me what to do or when to do it. The nurse was there consoling me and telling me that the baby was almost ready. I had finally dilated, as they said. Now it was time. I was hooked up to the baby heart monitor system and could hear the baby moving around and its heartbeat. I was ready to deliver. The doctor came in, and the pain hit its highest point. I could not take any more; I wanted to pass out. If this is what it feels like to have a baby, who would ever want to do this again? The pain went through my body and my head. It was horrible, the most unbearable pain one could ever go through. Much worse than abortion. The doctor set up my feet and asked me to move closer to him on the table with my legs wide open; again, I had a white sheet draped over me. I had been here before. For some reason, I became terrified. I could not see what the doctor was doing but could feel everything and hear him as he directed the nurses in the room and prepared my body for childbirth.

The doctor told me to "Push and breath." I did as he instructed. He told me to push more and breathe more. He continued, "Slow down, do not push now, breath, breath, breath. Push and breath." Ok, I did it all. I just wanted it out of me. The pain was even worst now. The heartbeat of the baby was so loud in my ear. It was horrible; too much going on; nurses running here and there, the doctor yelling orders at me. Then suddenly, the noise of the heart monitor stopped, but I still had to push and breathe. The baby was not out yet. The doctor finally said he could see the head and to keep pushing. "Push hard, push hard!" he was yelling at this point. I did as he instructed. Then I felt the rest of the baby plop right out between my legs. It felt like one big hard push, which was the head and the rest of the body. It felt like something very slimy just gushed out of my body in one push. It was like something foreign was released from your body all at once. This was done. The pain was gone instantly. I was in a state of shock for a moment from the pain and pushing. I could see the nurse running around the room. I was in a daze. The room was very hazy in sight.

My baby was dead.

The doctor told me that my baby was "DEAD!" I did not know what to do or say. I could not even ask why. It was horrible. All I could do was cry, cry, and cry. The doctor asked me if I wanted to hold the baby. I said, "Yes." The nurse brought my baby to me and handed him to me. Yes, it was a BOY. He was beautiful and looked just like my boyfriend's face on this little figure. He was so cute. But he had his eyes closed. He did not move, cry, or anything, just lying in my arms limp. I kissed him on his forehead and cried all the tears I could on his face. The nurse in the room watched as all this took place. She looked at me and came closer to the bed to take my son away from me. I could not let him go. She stopped her reach, and I cried and cried more tears on my son all over his face. He was wet from my tears. I was baptizing him in my tears; I did not realize that at the time. My thoughts were, why did this happen? Did my mother and sister wish this on me? I did not know what to think or do. I just held on. Then the nurse took him. Where was she taking him? He was stillborn. What and why?

The Visit

The first people I called were my boyfriend and his family. His mother answered the phone. I told her I had a baby boy and named him after his father. She was happy, but in the next voice, I told her that he was born dead. There was silence on the phone; a long silence came from her end. On my end, I was crying uncontrollably. She told me they were coming to the hospital to see me. My boyfriend was at work, and they would contact him for me. She told me to get some rest and that things will be alright.

My mother entered the room. She could see that I did not have my baby in the room with me. Who called her? She looked at me and asked me what I was going to do. She saw that I was crying uncontrollably. She did not even ask why. She asked again what I would do because I was not bringing that baby into her home. I said nothing. All I could do was cry. The nurse walked into the room. None of my siblings were there to visit me in the hospital room that day, only my mother. Again, she asked me in front of the nurse, "What are you going to do?" very impatiently. The nurse asked her who she was, and she told her my mother. The nurse asked her to come out of the room so that she could speak to her. I cried. I did not know how many tears I cried, but I could not stop. I tried, but it did not work. The nurse must have told my mother that my son was dead. She returned to the room and said, "Oh, your baby died, so you can come back home, and here are the rules." She told me that she forbids me to see my boyfriend ever again; he is not welcome in our house. She told me that I had to finish school and then get out of her house. I listened and cried some more. She left after laying down the rules. She hated me. If I could tell you, this chapter is one of the hardest

47

chapters of this book for me to write; trust me, they get worse. But this time in my life was all new. I did not know what to do about anything or anyone. I just did as she instructed.

My boyfriend's parents and his siblings arrived. His mother and sisters hugged me; his mother held me. Something I needed the most was a hug from a mother figure to let me know that life was not over for me. She told me that. I heard her whisper in my ear over and over, "you will be ok," as she held and rocked me to sleep. I was very tired and fell into a deep sleep.

When I awoke, my boyfriend was in a chair beside my bed, crying with his face in his hands. He was so upset, and I knew why. I touched his hand softly, and he looked at me. I had looked so worn out to him; he looked the same to me. I felt so sorry and bad for him. All I could think was that this was my entire fault because I hated the baby so much, and my family did too, especially my mother, who made this happen.

He assured me that it was not my fault. We cried so many tears together. It was a very sad scene. Nothing more to say about him throughout this story. He went on with his happy, secure life, and I was forgotten.

I was discharged from the hospital and returned to night school. His mother had returned all the baby gifts to the store. That was great, but my mind was playing so many recordings of the labor. My hearing of the baby's heartbeat was embedded in my ears. The doctor's yelling, pushing, and my body still appeared that I was pregnant. I was haunted over and over for years. My sister teased me for having a baby born dead. I was walking like a zombie. I was convinced that I deserved all I was getting from this day. My mother called me fat and ugly every day, and that was all I saw. I could not lose the baby fat soon enough. It took over a year to do so. It was horrible to look at the stretch marks, which were my physical reminder of the pain I endured over and over. Mentally, I wanted to end it all but did not know how or where. I thought of my son daily and how things would have been if he were alive. How he would have loved me, I would have loved him, and my boyfriend's family would show us love. But that would not happen now or ever. I was living what I deserved. I was not prepared or ready for what happened next. My boyfriend and I broke up; nothing new; I have been here before, loss after loss.

The cremation

The hospital contacted me to find out what I wanted to do with the baby's body. I did not know what to do or say. I called my grandpa and grandma. They would know what I should do. They took me to the hospital and spoke to the nurse and doctors for me. They contacted a funeral director, and we decided to have him cremated. The hospital let my grandparents and I see the baby one last time. My grandparents and I cried. They were speechless. They felt very sorry for me. I was unsure if they had ever seen a dead person so small before. I asked no questions, of course. After the tears, my grandfather prayed for the soul of the baby. I just bowed my head; I knew how to do that. Then we left the hospital. My grandparents took me back to their home. My grandma was so humble and nice. She told me how much they loved and cared for me, and they assured me that JESUS loves me and that she knew I had questions about why, but I should not question what happened. It was all supposed to happen. I listened and cried.

The funeral establishment cremated my son and gave me the urn with the ashes a month later. My grandparents took me there to pick up the urn. I opened it when I received it. It was a gold container with a wooden box bottom to it. It unscrewed from the bottom. It was a beautiful piece. Inside the urn was a clear plastic bag with my son's ashes. I opened it and was curious as to what they would feel like. I looked and could see baby bones in the ashes. I cried. My grandparents cried too. Before they took me home with my urn, my grandmother prayed for me and with me. I had to keep the urn away from my mother. I hid it on the top of the closet under some clothes, and sometimes, I would take it down at night and talk to him and then cry. So that was the extent of my closure. My boyfriend and his family just felt pity for me. We broke up for good.

Pregnancy #3

Just when you think that things could not get worse with being pregnant, they did. Now I was not pregnant by my boyfriend. He and I broke up soon after the baby died. Of course, I was the talk of the town. I was called every name in the book on the streets. My sister and I fought a lot at home and on the school bus. I was back in the day school for my last year. We would fist fight, and she would scratch up my face and embarrass me on the bus in front of all the kids. I hated her and myself and did not care what anyone was saying about me at this point.

I was the bitch that everyone called me, and I grew meaner and meaner. I was mean to everyone on the outside of my home. No one liked me, my mouth, or my actions. I had so many fights. I was the whore of the community and the neighborhood. I was having sex with this other boy from our town. I was having sex with him all the time. He just used me for sex, and I did the same. He did not like me at all. He just wanted to do things to me because I had freedom, and our mom worked at night. I would sneak out of the house and have sex with him. He taught me more things. One thing was that his manhood was much larger than anyone else I had sex with. He hurt my body at first, then my body got used to him. We had sex at his home and in our shed every chance I got.

I got pregnant again. My mother was pissed and was through with me now. She barely spoke to me, and when she did, it was nothing good or positive. No one knew but we that lived behind those closed doors. She was getting beaten by her lover repeatedly and going out partying; my problem was my problem at this point. I get what I deserve, she would say. But this time, my sister under me was pregnant at the same time. It was wonderful that she was pregnant. She could live at home with her boyfriend down the street, and everything was happy and lucky for her. Her boyfriend had a family and siblings, and everyone loved them in the hood. Well, my mother put me out. I found my own apartment and furnished it with secondhand furniture. I was on my own, struggling to survive for food and pay my bills. I was never taught how to do any of that at home; all I knew how to do was work. I was only seventeen.

I went into labor. Again, pain, suffering, and the baby heart monitor, but this time would be different. My female doctor sent me to a Philadelphia hospital for testing during the first six months of my pregnancy so that the same result would not happen again. There was no real cause of death on the death certificate of my first son. I hated myself and was disgusted that I had no boyfriend because, after the first showing of a big stomach, he did not speak to me again throughout the pregnancy. He said he heard on the street that I was having sex with another guy. This was not true. The guy he spoke of and I had not yet started having sex at that time. When my baby's father broke up with me, I turned to getting high off cocaine and drinking every chance I got. I snorted cocaine with some friends I met through a next-door neighbor; they were older. I did not care that I was pregnant, and the guy I got high with did not care either. I got high. All this took place after all the testing at the hospital. While in labor, I was scared and was reminded of all the nights I was high under the influence of cocaine and alcohol. I did not know what to do. All I knew was that here I go again. My mind was prepared this time for a dead baby because I had been there and done that, and I deserved what life had to offer to me at this point, and my mother's words ran in my ear repeatedly. Her words were embedded into the frame of my mind.

Ok, the baby came; the heart monitor did not stop this time. But they had to cut the baby out of me. I had to have a C-section. That was equally painful and gave a scar on my body as a reminder that I had a baby—no baby showers this time, no gifts, and no special day of love or anything.

This baby was different, very different.

The baby was a girl, or was it a boy born alive? I heard the baby cry out after the procedure. They cleaned the baby up, and then the nurse brought it to me, and my oldest sister was there with me in the hospital room. This baby was born on her birthday. She opened the blanket of the baby, and the face looked normal. I knew who the father of my baby girl and boy was. My constant sex partner, but he did not want to hear of it. But at this point, I did not care. My sister closed the baby blanket quickly. She looked at me; I had just awakened from a short nap. I was drugged up as they do to you in the hospitals in this condition following a C-section. I lay awake, and she said to me, "Look at the baby's body." I first looked at the baby's big head and face. Yup, his whole family has big heads, so it was his. This one looked "like me," my sister said, but I could not see that.

I opened the baby's blanket; nothing would prepare me at such a young age to what I saw. I thought that my eyes were deceiving me. The baby had six fingers on the right and left hand moving back and forth, six toes on each foot, and they moved. The baby had male and female sex organs. It had both, and the little wiener was sticking straight up, and it pissed on me, and under that was a vagina! The baby's body was paper thin and had a thin layer of skin. I could visibly see every organ inside the baby's body, like the bones and the veins; it was horrible to look at.

A freak was my thought. I closed the blanket as quickly as my sister had done before this moment. We looked at each other. The doctor came into the room and told me that the baby had a lot of complications and that they needed to do some tests on the baby to find out what went wrong. I thought to myself it was the drugs. I just knew it was the drugs. But I said nothing. I figured they would find out for themselves. The doctor told me that I would have to decide whether I wanted this baby to remain this way with the two sex organs or I would have to decide whether I wanted a boy or a girl. I had to decide that day so they could do what he had to do at the hospital for the baby. The nurse took my baby and left the room. I started crying uncontrollably. How could I make such a decision? What was I to do? I was totally clueless. My sister did not know what to do either; she was two years older than me. She left me to make the decision and left the hospital. I was in the room alone. So many thoughts flooded my mind like a rushing whirlwind. I did not know what to do or say. Why was all this happening to me? I do not know what to do with a baby with special needs; this was horrible. Such a horrible moment. I was only a teenager. What the hell is going on!?

The nurse and doctor returned to the room to tell me that my baby had lived for fifteen minutes and died. I was in shock.

I lay in my hospital bed alone and in shock. This is just not meant to be! This one would have been a real threat to my life. This was so horrible. I could not bear much more. I had to go home yet again with no baby to show for all the weight I gained, but I now had the scar to prove it. The old white devil doctor who performed the abortion made this so, or did he not?

The Stranger

A white man in a black robe entered my room. I thought to myself, who is he, and what does he want? The last thing I wanted to look at was a white man! I was upset. He walked over to my bed. I was too tired and upset to talk or even look at him. He touched my hand and asked, "Do you feel like jumping out of the hospital window?" I thought, here we go again. The devil himself is here to take me with him. I moved my hand from his touch and told him, "I did not kill myself after my first born; why would I do it now?" My voice was very stern. I turned my face from his and turned my head, and when I looked back briefly, he was gone! Where did the guy go? Who was he? And I did not even hear his shoes move toward the door? It was one strange moment in time; I remember well. I thought about that for years to come. The nurse soon reentered the room. They were moving me from the maternity ward to a regular room in the hospital so that I would not hear the other babies crying. But little did she know that I heard my baby cry, and for years later, in dreams and while awake in a world all alone, I could still hear that baby's cry.

Sex Addiction

I got well, left the hospital, and headed home to a life of smoking weed and having sex with multiple partners. Now I was an expert in every sex act and was willing to do any position. I had many boys looking for me to have sex with them. None wanted to like or love me; I was too mean. The important thing to remember here is that they did not choose me; I chose them. I selected every one of my partners. I knew in the first five minutes of meeting if I was going to have sex with them or not. All I did was have sex. There was no girl out there better, and I knew it. It was all unprotected too. We know what came with unprotected sex was a variety of sexually transmitted diseases, and when I upgraded from boys to men, it became even better. I had married men chasing me. I teased them. They paid for my BMW payment, rent, clothes, and everything else I wanted. All I had to do was live out the name of whore, trick, freak, and some.

But I did not care. It was not love, and no one was going to show me love. I figured I got what I wanted through sex. I did it day and night. It was great but came with many consequences. I fought wives, baby mamas, and men who wanted it, and I was not giving it to girlfriends who would come to my door or want to fight me in the streets. But I could fight. I earned my name and lived up to every one of them. I partied, got high off weed and cocaine, and had sex. I even tried opium and hallucinating drugs one time. I hung around the bad crowd who got high. I watched guys shoot up heroin and then fall asleep. I watched people and joined in with them smoking cocaine through a pipe. I had even more sex every which way when I was high, front, back, up, down, and sideways; all I wanted to do was be pleased. I was taught by real grown-up men how to please them in new ways. It felt much better to me having sex with men than with boys. Boys reached an orgasm fast, and men took their time, which was a new level of ecstasy for me. I was being talked about all over town and in the hood. I stopped having sex there and started having sex out of town. My girlfriends used to ask me what they could do new to please their men. That's how great I was at sex. I was a professional in positions, flexible, and would let the man have me in any way.

What a mighty web we weave. I was falling deeper and deeper into the life of being a sex addict, and I was mean. I took nothing from anyone. I never smiled. I had fun with my girlfriends, drank, and danced all night at parties and clubs. I was attractive. My body and hair were always fly. My body was the measurements of a true brick house. Perfect 36-24-36, and the ass and hips grew larger with certain sex positions. The backside grew, and my waist did not. So, you can see now how I was attracting men. I had no time for boys or anyone hanging around for a long time. When I was done with you and your manhood, I had two minutes to say "next." I kept it moving, especially if I did not get what I wanted.

Pregnancy # 4

It took place, and yet I lost another child. The story never changed. This time, by an old flame who was in the military. He said he was into me, but he had a girl in the military, so no love was lost. I lost the baby, so I thought he would not care anyway. Years later, I told him, but he did not care then or now just like I said.

To this day, I still have no children. But I did not give up trying. I left the baby there at the hospital, not knowing what to do with it. I did not bother to name this one. I did not want to bother my grandparents with yet another voice of pain. I cried my usual tears, which were something I did daily when alone. Mourning was my life.

Only my family knew how mentally messed up I was, but physically, I looked good. Just like the baby that almost threatened my life, living 15 minutes, the face was normal and cute, but I opened the blanket, and the truth was revealed. All my hidden secrets were bottled up inside. I had to move back home at age 18; yes, with all that happened, I was only 18 years old. It seemed like a lot to go through. My mother was livid, but she and I knew that baby would not make it, so once it died in the hospital, she made me get my tubes tied. The doctors sat her and me in a room and explained the procedure. She was only there because I was not old enough for the procedure. You had to be 21 years of age at that time. I told her I did not want to go through with it, and she was pissed.

As you know, I did as she instructed, just as an enslaved person would. Here I go again with the white doctors, I told myself. They told us that it would not be permanent and that it was a new procedure that they would do that would just tie knots in the tubes on each end and that they would come untied in five years if I wanted at that time to decide to have children. My mother signed the papers that day and forced me to sign as well. Little did I know that I was a test patient that day.

The procedure was done, and I went home. I had a form of birth control, my tubes were tied, and I would never have to worry about a baby, pregnancy, and wondering who the baby's father was now. Things should be good for at least five years, or so I thought. I left the hospital without a care in the world. My mother was content with knowing that I would not be an embarrassment to her in the future. She held the secret.

I continued with my whorish ways and was mean as a rattlesnake.

My grades had dropped in school; however, I graduated from high school. Now was time for me to get out once again per my mother. I yet got another apartment; I was working and saving money the men gave me. I found a very nice place. Although it was small, I knew how to keep a place clean. I got a job at the toy factory and purchased a car. I was living well, or so I thought. This way of so-called free living came with much drama, such as fights and stalking from different men. I was doing adult things and going through adult consequences. I was not ready for all of this; I just wanted to have fun. Mentally, I was becoming a terror, and, in my car, I was a terror on wheels. Physically I was the bomb, body and hair flowing just the way it all needed to be. I worked hard for a living and took whatever else I could get. I struggled with relationship after relationship. I was now getting older and just wanted to have fun. I was at every party and wore what I needed to get what I wanted each night. I selected who and did what I wanted with them. The men did not control me; I controlled them.

Most men were after me from the age of 17 to 50.

CHAPTER 8

AFTER THOUGHT

I can only pray that the last chapters painted a clear picture of reality to anyone pregnant, agreeing to an abortion and using drugs, and the psychological effects it all had on me. Does this happen to everyone using drugs while pregnant? I do not know. I can only tell you what happened to my babies and me. It was a horrifying moment in my life. I went about each pregnancy irresponsibly. I only thought of myself and my mother and did not even give my child a chance to live and to be loved. Nothing can replace the love a real mother has when carrying a child in her womb. The child grows and becomes a special part of you. I remember each time feeling the baby move and stretch. I remember craving foods that I still do not eat today. But you, as parents, pregnant teens, and fathers, please pay attention. Prevent this from happening to your children. Education and love are the keys.

If just one person could read my story and learn that drugs, alcohol, and low self-esteem are aids that kill unborn babies.

What a threat that one baby would have been to me. Would I have been able to make the right decision regarding the sex? Would my child be a freak like me?

Many parents hide the fact that their children are born with problems. When using drugs while pregnant, a host of things could happen worse than what I experienced. The child could have lived. The child would have suffered along with me. Looking at that child would have reminded me of my hidden mistakes for the rest of my life. The mistakes I made while doing drugs and alcohol during my pregnancy are right there. I already had the scar; that was enough for me. I still see it every day. Having unprotected sex with different men was not a smart decision either. The spiritual bonds are also deadly to your life and life journey. We need to do what my grandmother used to tell us girls at a very young age, "Watch who you have your children by." That is real!

The pains at that time made me want to change my life. I felt that my life was in the mode of self-destruction. I did not have anyone to turn to. What do I do now? All my children were dead, and all I could ask was why.

Mothers and fathers, please talk to your teens about abstinence, drugs, alcohol, sex, using protection, and relationships. Talk about the love that you have for them. Otherwise, they may have a story like mine when you pass away. Why not talk to them now? Secrets are not good, the basement parties are not good, sex in unfamiliar places inside and outside buildings, and in parked cars is not good. Please do not let your children fend for themselves in these last and evil days. Let them know you are there for them in their time of need. Men, fathers, you are equally responsible and extremely important.

Otherwise, your grandchildren will turn out evil, deformed or worst, that child could live. Would you then deny your grandchild? The hood, fake family members, and jealous siblings who laugh at you behind closed doors and speak curses and whispers behind your back will take a toll on your young lives. What changes and decisions will you make today?

CHAPTER 9

THE RELATIONSHIP

I was now 26 years old, with a beautiful apartment in Philadelphia, working at a bank for a few years, going and attending community college; bad things were behind me.

Although I had other men I saw throughout the years, none were significant until now. I was seeing a man in another state, I was in love. He was tall, and very handsome; my cup of tea and would come and spend time with me on his days off and on the weekends, I would spend time at his place. By this time, we had been together for four years, and things were going well.

He got hurt on his job and was a very important person in his community. This man had an unfortunate accident on his job and required surgery. We talked, and I decided to move in with him to help him through his surgery and to care for him, I moved all my things, a beautiful white living room set, a white dining room set, and a white bedroom set, all very nice and elegant, to his home, I moved all my clothes, shoes, and everything else I owned.

I got in my sports car and drove to my new home and location. All was going well for the first year I was living there he had to be out of work longer than expected due to his rehabilitation process. I cared for him through this his recuperation as well. His friends would come around to visit. Some flirted with me and some did not, some were loyal to him, and little did he know there was one who was not. But I never told him. Life went on I did as I was asked to do while caring for and driving him around. On his road to recovery, I found out that he was seeing another girl behind my back who was a part of his recovery treatment. I once overheard him on the phone; we had our first fight ever. He pushed me to the floor when I approached him, and I was shocked since he had never laid a hand on me before this day.

On one sunny day, I saw one of his male friends or so-called friends on the street while I was shopping. He was the one who told me about this girl. I would meet with him, and we would give me updates. He told me what my man was doing at the time behind my back. I had not messed around or ever cheated on my man. When I returned home one day, I saw this girl in our home. She was sitting in the living room on my white sofa. I asked her who she was since I had not seen my man any place in the house at that moment. My man came out of the kitchen, and I asked him who she was since she had not answered my question. He told me that she was "his friend." I questioned, "What kind of friend because I have never seen her before?" I knew most, if not all his so-called friends, male and female. This guy knew a lot of people.

He said his "special friend", I asked her to leave and he told her to stay and that this was his house, and I could leave if I did not like it. He turned his back to walk away, and I followed him into the kitchen. She sat in the living room with her drink and could hear our loud argument. I was pissed and cursing, and he accused me of messing with one of his friends. I reminded him that if I wanted to have sex with his friend with my history, I would have done it by now and more than once. But I had not done so. He did not believe me.

We argued, and he pushed me over a chair that was in the dining room. He was six foot four inches and easily weighed at least three hundred pounds. He was huge, and he was mad. I experienced at that moment just how strong he was. I fell over the chair. I went back into the kitchen and tried to fight him. He punched me in my face, blackened my eye, took me by my neck, and flung me across the room. He then picked me up, tossed me toward the door, and told me to get out of his house. I said, "Not without my things." He told me I had twenty-four hours to get my things out. This was our first fight. I had never seen this side of him before. He was a woman beater. I got that now and have never seen it coming. You think you know someone, but you really do not.

I got into my little car and drove to the nearest phone booth to call my mother. She answered the phone. I told her my man had just beaten me up and thrown me out of his house. She said, "You made your bed, you better lie in it," then hung up. I guess she was an expert since she was beaten most of the time by her lover when we were young. We saw him hit and abuse her. My siblings and I saw her bruises that she covered up and heard her cry many times in the dark. This was nothing, and she had already told us that we would never be able to move back home. It was raining outside and I had no more money. All I did was hang up the phone. I saw the bruises on my face and body in the reflection of the phone in the booth. I cried and did not know what to do now but to sleep in my sports car.

I went back the following day to get my clothes. The girl was gone, he opened the door, and he was cold and told me to get my things. I told him, "I have no place to go. I will take my clothes and come back later for my furniture." He said that was ok. He understood I was new to the area and did not know too many places because I was taking care of him. I had no money saved because I did not have to work. I stuffed all my clothes in my sports car, and that was it: my clothes, perfumes, toiletries, and jewelry. I could not fit anymore or anything else in the small car, I left. I did not know where to go and was officially homeless. The first thing I knew was that I had to find work. I tried to put in applications. I bathed in the McDonald's bathrooms early in the mornings after sleeping in my car at night. I did that each morning until the manager told the other homeless people and me that they were locking the doors and that we could not come to wash in their sinks or rest up there anymore.

I had to find another location to camp out since I had not yet found a job. I found a newspaper company that printed newspapers in the next town and used their lot to park and live in my car. It felt safe and was well-lit. The Security Officer would let me park my car there on his shift. It was great. The following day, I would go to a different McDonald's in the next town and wash, then dress before going out to look for a job, which was unsuccessful. The security guy was fired, so I could no longer park my car in the newspaper lot. There was some new officer at that location, but he was not so nice. I drove around as it was getting dark and found a motel. I saw an Indian lady outside. I pulled over and asked her if they had rooms for rent. I had no money, but I did not tell her. I needed a place to sleep, shower, and iron my clothes. I ran out of choices at this point. She said yes. I went in and filled out the paperwork and then told me that it would be fifty dollars a week! I was broke. I told her I had no money and that I just started a new job and had not gotten paid yet. My pay would be the following Monday. At least I would have a place to sleep over the weekend. She went into a back room, and her husband appeared before me. I had to explain the story to him. I used a fake name and told him about getting beaten up and not having identification. He took down my tag number and let me rent a room for a week. He never checked my tag for the real name. He gave me my room key. I went into my room and looked around. It smelled badly; it was not the best of places, but I had no choice. It had a bed and half decent shower with a tub; it was perfect for now.

I had been sleeping in my car for three weeks and my back ached. A few days went by. I would get up, shower, and drive around looking for work, then go back in. I had all my clothes hanging up in the hotel closet, and I would go to Burger King and similar places to get food out of the trash that people would throw away and take it back to my room to eat it cold. It was horrible, but it cured hunger pains. One day, I returned to my room, and the door was half broken where the doorknob key entry was. I did not have to put in the key to open the door. Someone had broken into my motel room and stolen all my clothes and everything else I had. I went to the owner, who I never did pay, and told his wife. She sent him to look at the room. He told me that I had to pay to live there. I was upset. I told him I had no money yet and that I needed my clothes for work! We argued and I started crying. He and his wife felt bad for me. They called the cops, and with that came trouble.

The officer who wrote up a report looked familiar and asked if I looked familiar to him; he replied no. I said nothing and instantly thought about the punch in the face and knocking me over the chair incident, this was all upsetting. Things I wanted to forget about came back to the surface of my mind. Once the officers left, one man stayed on the scene. I was crying and he came over to me and whispered, "What are you even doing here?" Apparently, this was a motel for prostitutes! I had no clue. "I have no place to go," was my response. I was visibly upset, which meant nothing to him.

The motel had two sides. The other side of the motel was safer because it faced the side streets. The motel owner and his wife were compassionate and felt bad about me being robbed of everything I had owned. I had nothing but the clothes on my back. The familiar officer then walked into the motel front lobby area with me to retrieve the key for my new room. He spoke to the owner and paid for me to live there for three months. He figured this would be enough time for me to get a job and move out. It was a good thing, so I thanked him, and he left. I never saw the hotel owner give him a key to my room. I went to the new room, sat on the bed paranoid now, and feared retaliation from the prostitutes, which now I noticed them going in and out. I had never noticed all the activity at night because I would search for a job during the day and come back to the room before nightfall and would never come back out of the room. Well, someone was watching and robbed me during the day when things were quiet. I sucked up the tears, or at least I tried to suck up the tears that continued to flow freely. I sat in this smelly room with the dirty blue carpet. The bed smelled, cloudy white sheets that looked dirty, and the bathroom had cracked tiles and roaches. The room was dark because the curtains were closed. I sat alone and in the dark. I was so upset, thinking at the time, how did I get here? Not meaning here in this place, I knew why I was there. I got what I deserved, and that rang true from my mother's embedded voice ringing in my ears, "You made your bed, you better lie in it." This was the bed. How did I allow myself to get into this type of relationship? Were there any warning flags? This was a new change for me. I did not like it. I had no money, just a room for a few months. Now knowing this is a hooker joint, I thought this place was the lowest of the lowest and smelled bad.

I got up from bed, took a shower, and then cried.

CHAPTER 10

THE RAPE

I t was 3:00 am, and I was sound asleep when I heard the door of the motel room open. I was in a daze when I saw the light from the parking lot fill the dark room. I immediately jumped out of bed. I was sleeping with my clothes on. There was a familiar male voice that filled the space. The voice was deep, and he said, "Hey," and he closed the door behind him. I turned on the light. My ex had a key!!! I asked him, "How did you get the key to my room?" He said he got it from a friend the day he paid for the room." I told him he had no right here and to leave or I would leave. He walked his huge body closer and closer to me and tried to kiss me. I did not want him to kiss me. I moved out of the way. I was almost in the corner of the room. I continued to move about the room, trying to escape his horrible kisses. Now I was next to the large motel room mirror and the sink. He pushed me to the left of that area into the corner. This was not a place I wanted to be. The sink counter was under by the bottom of the mirror and to the right of me was a silver bar on the wall that held the towels. Now I was cornered, I thought to myself. This guy is too strong to fight; I knew that from the previous fight about a month ago. He stood firm in front of me. I was scared.

He took me by my neck and lifted me with one hand. He put his mouth to mine and kissed me hard. I did not want his tongue in my mouth; I shut my mouth tightly. He bit the bottom of my lip, and it was so hard it swelled immediately and started bleeding. I scratched and punched his face, and it did not even bother him. He then put me down and punched me in the face so hard I saw stars before my eyes. I was dazed and felt the right side of my face begin to swell. I fell over the counter and then tried to kick out at him with both my legs and strength. He grabbed my right leg and started to drag me to the bed my head now hit the counter, and I fell hard to the floor, hurting my back because that area was a tile floor and then I could feel my back on the carpet. I was kicking my left leg at him, trying to get him to let me go he took me to the bed, ripped my pants, and then turned me over and ripped the back side of my pants. I was fighting all the way. I was kicking and telling him, "NO!" and to stop, but no one came to help. I then knocked the lamp onto the floor. Now only a little bit of light filled the room, only a shadow on the ceiling my face was swollen; the back of my head hurt so badly, and my vision was blurred, but I could see his ugly black face. It was horrible. He looked like a big angry ape. I was horrified he was extra strong as I grew weaker and weaker for fighting and getting nowhere. He held my hands and arms down. I was so tired at this time from the fighting I just gave in.

My ex had ripped my pants, which were my only pair and did not even take off my panties, but he ripped my shirt buttons, and the top of the collar on my shirt was ripped. My shirt was now fully open, and my bra and breast were exposed he then told me that he loved my body and my ass. He flipped me over, held onto my arms by the elbow, and held me down on my right side. His body weight was sitting on the back of my legs. He felt like he weighed at least five hundred pounds. This man was so heavy my legs were tired and weak and now hurt so badly. I was sore all over; he removed my shirt and told me he would punch me in the back of my head if I moved. I did not move; I had no strength left. Once he took off my shirt, I was not prepared for what was going to happen next.

As I lay on my stomach and he sat on the back of my legs, my big round ass was exposed. He pulled down my panties. I could hear but could not see him; of course, I knew in my mind that he was unbuckling his belt around his protruding stomach, I heard him unzip his zipper, and the room got very quiet time seemed to stand still. Nothing could have prepared me for what was going to happen next. He pulled me by my hair from the back, yanked my head back so hard I could not scream; I thought he was going to break my neck. He then had his knee in my back as he pulled one leg out of his pants. A thousand thoughts ran through my mind, and they were all horrible. Thoughts like, is he really going to rape me? Is he really going to hurt me this way? What was I doing with this animal in the first place? Is he serious? Is he really going to do this, rape really? Those thoughts played over and over in my mind. It was horrifying. I had to get off this bed. But he had me held down, I could not move, and with my head back this far, I could not scream. Now he had both legs out of his pants; I could not see anything. All I could do was close my eyes as tears streamed out of my swollen face. I could not even swallow at this point. My throat hurt badly from screaming and his big hands around my throat at the beginning of the fight. I did not know what to do. I had no fight left in me and tried to muster up a way to get out of this hold, but I saw nothing at this point, nothing but pain filled my head. Every muscle in my body was exhausted but what I knew was that hate was love.

I thought this was a man who loved me. Now he hated me, or was he showing me love? This was the worse position to be in: helpless, hopeless, and thoughtless. I could feel him release his one knee on my back and still had his hand locked on my hair from the back of my head. I was so sore and crying for him to please stop. I attempted to voice those pleads from the base of my sore and raw throat. He heard nothing; he took his hard manhood and forced it into my anus! I could not even scream. It hurt so badly. It was not moist or anything, just dry and hurt so badly. Let me tell you that it was the worse pain of any pain I had ever had in my life up to this point. I had childbirths and an abortion, but this pain was the worst.

I cried out with a brief gargle. He moved in and out of my asshole, which must have felt good to him. This seemed to go on for eternity. My body shook with severe pain. He knew I was hurting, but it seemed to turn him on more because my anus would tense up as he moved violently in and out of my body. My body went into shock. I relaxed beyond my control, and my body stopped tensing up immediately. I laid there like a rag doll. I had been the lap dog, one of the devil's trolls, suicidal at one point, and now a rag doll, adding on to the many names I had lived out and had become over the years.

My thoughts were none. My life flashed before my tearful eyes. I blanked out of my thoughts. It hurt too much to even think. But I knew it had to be over soon enough. I just wanted him to finish and get out. The night was endless. After that pain, he was just getting started. He then turned me over and lay on top of me, and I just laid there with my eyes closed, tears streaming down my face uncontrollably. My entire face felt like it was enflamed and was swollen. I could not even move my lips, and my throat was very sore. I lay on my back, and he pulled open my legs and began forcing himself on me from the front. He laid his entire weight on my body, and he felt like a ton at this point. He forced his manhood in and out repeatedly. I did not move any part of my body. He finally finished, got dressed, and left saying nothing at all. I could not move my entire body inside and out from head to toe and was in pain.

I lay there in the half-lit room and cried until there were no more tears. I must have fallen asleep finally.

THE NEXT MORNING

I noticed that it was daylight. I looked for my watch on the bed table, and it was gone! My car keys were gone! The motel clock, radio, and phone were gone! I was upset that I even woke up at all. I wanted to just die. But when I went to move off the bed, my body and head ached. My anus hole and vaginal area were so sore that I did not know what was going on. I could barely lift my arms. I forced myself up off the bed, moving slowly. I went to the bathroom and noticed myself in the mirror. The right side of my face was so swollen and now black and blue, my bottom lip was swollen and sore, and I could see his teeth marks on the bottom part of my lip. My arms had black and blue marks from being held down. My body was sore, my hair was all over my head, and my head hurt badly. I tried to remove my bra, something he had not removed, but I could not reach my arms behind my back. When I went to take the strap from my arms, I could not lift my arm to remove my bra. I gave up. I turned to the side and saw the bruises on my back and a scratch on the top of my anus area just below my hip. I could not see the bruises on the back of my knees; I could only feel them when I bent to sit on the toilet seat to pee. I moved slowly and was still in a state of shock. I had no thoughts; I just saw with my eyes. This had to all be a dream. Until I went to pee; it hurt so bad that I wanted to scream but felt that my throat was sore when I tried to swallow. I went to wipe myself from front to back and felt that my entire private area was swollen to the touch. It was hot and swollen. I had never felt this pain before now. I went to reach around and wipe the back side of my anus. My anus was also swollen. I was in so much pain, and all I could do was cry. I was so upset. I could not move my body to get off the toilet. I was stuck in this sitting position, and my private parts felt heavy, like they were falling out.

Finally, after a while, I forced myself to get up. It was so uncomfortable sitting there. I tried hard to replay where I went wrong. The rape filled my thoughts, and the pain filled my mind and body over and over. I was physically and mentally reminded of the pain of the most recent events. I moved slowly to the other side of the room to get my clothes off the floor, what was left of them anyway. I picked up my pants from the end of the bed they were ripped, my panties were ripped too, so I could not put them on. My shirt, which was now on the floor, was difficult to reach but also ripped.

I tried to see if I could put it back together but could not. I pulled the dirty, smelly blanket I did not want to touch from the bed, put it over my body, and went for the door. I reached for the knob, and the door would not open! I looked out the window to see why the door was not opening but could not see the door itself from the side window. I looked and saw no one in sight, no housekeeper or anyone else. I looked through the large window and tried punching on the window in a frantic state, and no one was there. I was locked in this room!

My head began to scream out. My arms and hands were even sorer from knocking on the window and banging on the door, hoping to be heard. How was I locked in this room? I went back to use the phone, but he had taken the phone. There was no phone in the room. Are you serious? I was so upset. I sat on the bed and cried; that seemed to be all that I could do. Even my tears had pain. Throughout that day, I went back and forth to the window. I figured since my body was sore, I should take a warm bath. Maybe it would help me relax and think about how I could get out of this room. I slowly walked to the bathroom and ran warm water into the tub. It took forever for me to get into the tub to sit, but I was able to do so. I spent what seemed like an eternity in the tub. The water felt good to my body, especially my private parts. Although it was hard for me to sit on my bottom, my anus started to feel a little calmer. The swelling I could feel was still there in both areas. The warm heat of the water was soothing. My body began to calm down from the severe pain.

The beating and rape were still on my mind. I cried and cried. I splashed water on my face repeatedly; it felt much better. The black and blue marks on my body and face reminded me of the pain, but the water felt good, like it was a tonic to my soul that had now been battered. But I knew I got what I deserved. My suffering was long, and I had to endure this too. It was all my fault, I thought. The tub water began to get cold. I turned on the water to warm it back up. I sat in the tub until my bones began to allow me to move a little more freely. I rubbed my face softly with water over and over to get the swelling to go down. My face started to feel better.

I finally got out of the tub. I took the towel and tried to dry off softly and slowly without pressure. My body had cooled off, and I started to feel pain once again. I looked in the mirror, hoping that the water wiped away the bruises, swelling, and rape, but the trauma was still there as I looked. I looked horrible. I put water on my hair. I had no comb or brush because it was all stolen when the prostitutes robbed my room. I used the water from the sink and my fingers to groom my hair. I used the conditioner from the small container left in a room drawer to make it soft and to be able to move my finger through my hair. I tried to get it all to go to the back to put in a ponytail. My head hurt so badly, so that was hard to do. But I was able to manage to do just that. I had the worst headache. I moved slowly back to the window with the towel around me. I looked out, and no one was there. I felt not only alone but deserted. I went to sit back on the bed and was very tired and defeated. I lay back down and figured I could watch TV. I looked on the dresser, and there was no TV. I did not even notice the night before that the room had no TV, or did my ex take the TV like he did the phone? It was too hard to even think, so I just lay down on the bed and fell asleep in the dark, cold place.

THE PRISONER

Early in the wee morning hours, the door was opened again. I was awakened again by this monster. I told him, "No, and please leave." I told him to let me go, and I will never come there again. I begged him to let me leave. He told me that he paid for the room and he could come here anytime he wanted and that he had a lock outside the door so that he could come and get what he wanted from me until he was done with me when the room time was up. So now I thought that I must endure this for months. I would not let that happen. I was getting out somehow. Again, I tried to fight him off me, but it was much easier for him this time because all I had on was my bra and a towel. He pulled the towel off as I tried to get up from the bed. I made it to the floor; he was over me on the floor and slapped me with his open right hand. My face was on fire! I saw stars. It was already swollen and sore; now, it was pain on top of pain. I held my face and pleaded with him, "Please stop! I am tired," I cried and tried to scream with a scratchy throat.

He now had me on the floor. I was bare at the bottom, and he was excited. He pulled my legs roughly and forced himself on me right there on that dirty rough carpet. I had rug burns from him forcing himself in and out. He did not even take off his pants this time, his manhood was out, and his huge heavy belt buckle hit my stomach area between him and me. He laid his heavy body on me and tried to kiss me on my bruised lips. He saw what he did to my face, and I begged him to stop, but my cries went unheard by him or anyone else. He finally finished his business and pulled me from the floor. I was just crying. He pulled me by my hair to the chair in the room and handcuffed me to the chair with my right hand and left hand around the wood piece on the back of the chair. My arms were so sore in this position, and now my hands were held together; even my shoulder muscles were sore from him stretching my arms.

I was tied to this chair, and my private area was so sore and swollen I could barely sit. He said, "Shut up! You're getting what you deserved for how you acted in my home in front of my girlfriend." I told him, "I am so sorry, and if you let me go, I will never do it again. I will leave and never come back, and you will never see me again." I promised and begged like a dog would for food. I cried and pleaded, and he said he did not believe me and would let me go when he was ready. I had not eaten in three days now and was hungry and very thirsty. He told me to keep quiet and stop crying and that I looked ugly. He moved the chair from the area of the bed and moved it to the bathroom, and closed the door so I could not be heard. I did not even think that this chair would fit into the bathroom; it did not. So, he then moved it with me tied to it between the bathroom door and the sink area. He called me a whore, a bitch, and a trick and threatened to treat me like that every time he came in the room. He said he was going to take what he wanted. He also said he would bring me food and something to drink.

I just sat there sore and in severe pain. My head hurt so badly that I was helpless, and it was a hopeless cause for me to try to fight any longer. I should just take what I deserved. He left the room. I could hear that he had a lock or something outside the door. I sat and cried. I did not know what else to do but cry. The chair was so uncomfortable, and my arms were numb from the pain of being stretched. The room was cold and damp and smelled terrible. I tried my best to get comfortable but could not.

The monster returned once again. This time he had food with him. It was Chinese food. It had egg in it, and I hated the taste of eggs, but I will eat anything right now. He came over to me after entering the room. I sat up in fear now. The monster told me to calm down and that he was not here to do anything to me, just to feed me. He opened the bag and stuck the spoon in the white container after opening the top, and I watched and said nothing to him. He leaned against the counter in front of the mirror; he was one big ape to me. I hated him at this point. But I dare not say anything; he looked at me with the food container in one hand and the plastic spoon in the other hand. I sat still, mouthwatering from the smell of the food. He looked down at me and said I was an ugly whore and a bitch once again. I said nothing. He used his foot to move the chair closer to him. He then took the spoon and forced it into my mouth, which was swollen and sore. I guess I was not opening my mouth fast or wide enough, then he threw the next spoonful at my face. He asked if I was thirsty. I said yes, and he had a cup of iced tea from the Chinese place on the counter by the sink. He gave me a sip of tea, only a brief sip. Then he asked me if I wanted more. I said nothing, just looked at him in anger. He knew I was pissed, but one eye was closed from the beating the previous day.

He called me a whore, unbuckled his pants, and zipped down his zipper. He then felt for his manhood, put it in his right hand, began to fondle himself in front of me, and told me that if I closed my eyes, he would punch me in the head. He threatened that if I moved my head in any way, he would pull my hair out of my head. I was so scared I watched while he fondled himself, and it grew before my face and was at its peak of hardness in front of me. This evil man stood before me and told me he would allow me to eat if I sucked his dick. I could barely open my mouth, my lip was sore, my throat was sore, and my neck was sore. He asked if I was hungry and thirsty. I again said yes. He gave me more tea and told me to stick out my tongue. I tried my best to get my tongue through my swollen lip. It appeared before his manhood which was hard and close to my mouth. He stood before me, moved his leg on each side before me, and bent his body to have his manhood directly in front of me.

He poured the tea over my face, which hit my tongue, face, and his manhood. It was wet before me; he made me lick it. I did as told as I have done so many years before. Here I go again, living up to the name of a lap dog. I was now officially a lap dog. I hated myself more with every lick. Getting what "I deserved" as my mother's voice rang in my head. I learned this well. I licked; he forced his manhood into my mouth. I could barely open my mouth, but he managed to get it in slowly, but he was now standing before me. I thought of biting his manhood off, but he would kill me in this room and no one would even know. I could not die this way, I thought. I licked and sucked. He poured more and more tea in my face so that my mouth would not dry out his manhood which he stayed in position, sliding back and forth inside and outside of my mouth. He was feeling good, I could tell because of the sounds coming from his mouth. He did this until he reached an orgasm all over my face; it was in my eye, mouth, cheeks, and tongue. He was done now. I knew he would free me.

He wiped my face roughly with a wet towel and then said he wanted some pussy. I was so defeated and humiliated; I said nothing, as always. I sat there waiting for food. He left the food and the rest of the tea on the counter. By this time, the room was dark. He left the room, locking the door from the outside. I was in complete darkness and alone. It was quiet. I tried to move the chair up by trying to lift my body and move the chair with my weak legs. The chair was super heavy, and my arms hurt so badly, but I wanted the food on that counter. I could not see but could try to feel with my chin as I moved the chair forward like, maybe an inch or so. I felt the food container and tried to get it to turn over so I could eat it from the counter. I felt the container fall to the floor at my feet. I started to cry. I tried to reach it with my feet but was moving the container away from me instead of closer. I gave up. I was also thirsty and tried to reach for the tea. I was able to get it to the right side of my face on the counter in the dark. Once the container was on the right side, I could get it turned over and feel the tea on the counter wet under my chin. I lay my face to the side and used my tongue to lap up the tea from the counter. It was not much, but it did wet my tongue, and I was able to swallow; it was soothing to the mouth.

I tried to stand up and move the chair, but it was too heavy for my arms. I tried to bend over, but that was impossible because of the pain I felt throughout my body. I felt defeated and just sat there in the dark and cried myself to sleep in the chair of bondage. His actions went on for over a month. No one ever came to my room, no housekeeper or anyone. I did not and could not understand why. He once came in the middle of the night, took the handcuffs off, and forced me to suck his manhood. He forced his manhood into my anus on more than what seemed like thousands of occasions. He would beat, slap, and throw food and drink at me. He would also run my bath water because he saw how swollen my private parts would get and force me to sit in very hot water in the tub. I could barely get one foot in the water because it was so hot. He would see me struggling, punch my head, and push me into the tub of hot water. I would scream so loud, but no one came to my rescue.

This lasted for a while longer. He once bought another one of his friends into the room and they both forced themselves on me and made me do so many sexual acts on them both. The sex was unprotected. The new guy had a stick of some sort in his hand, and my ex was making me suck his manhood. This one particular time, while I was doing so, I was made to get on all fours while the other guy would be forcing himself in me from behind. He would hit me on my anus so hard with this stick and pull my hair from the back of my head. He snatched at my hair so hard that it would make the ex's manhood come out of my mouth. My ex would get mad at me and punch me in the face while this other guy was forcing himself into my private area. Then he would stop and let my ex beat me and call me names. I just lay there, and they both told me to get on all fours. I did so, crying and shedding many tears. He and the new guy were whispering while looking at my bottom, which turned them on by just looking at it in this position. My ex told me to spread my legs and put my face on the bed. I did so all bruised up. My body was in so much pain.

Nothing prepared me for what was going to happen next. The new guy pushed the stick up my anus so far that I thought I would pass out in pain. He left it there for what seemed like an hour. But it was only for a few minutes. I screamed so loud they were both laughing at me. I cried and fell to my stomach, and he pulled it out. I had never felt such pain in my entire life, even during childbirth. My ex ran bath water and I got in the tub of hot water. This time, it was not very hot, just warm. Once in the tub, the new guy came into the bathroom. They had been drinking beer and liquor they had brought with them for the party they were having on my behalf. I sat naked in the tub; my body was so sore I wanted to die. I thought dying would be better than living another day of this pain. I then started thinking of ways of just ending it all. If they left the liquor bottle, I would cut my wrist. I knew they would be done with me if they put me in the tub, so they would me leaving soon.

I waited in pain with all my thoughts of suicide and tried to clean myself up as instructed. My ex came in to help me with soap on my back and told me to stand up and he washed me between my bottom cheeks, which were swollen, and the touch was causing more pain. I cried out; it hurt. He made me sit back down. I sat, and he washed me all over. He asked his friend if he wanted to bathe me. The new guy came in, started to fondle his manhood in front of me, and then pissed all over my hair. I was so upset I could not even get through this chapter to write such a horrible and terrifying act of hate. This is truly a hate crime. But I was going to commit suicide when they left my room. I had a plan for the first time.

After he pissed in my hair, he pushed my head to the water and held down my back which was so sore. Then my ex came in, and he told him he pissed on me, and they were laughing. My ex turned on the shower water and washed my hair. After some time, he ex told me to get out of the tub and dry off. I did so. I thought it was a matter of time and this life would be over. I began to cry, but he was pissed and slapped my face. He told me to "shut up." I sucked it up as I had done many times before. I dried off my body lightly, and he gave me a tee shirt and panties that he had in a bag along with some clothes that I had apparently left at his house that his new girlfriend had found and was going to throw in the trash. I was happy to have on clothes, but it was thongs that were very painful to even put on. However, I had to cover up while they both watched me get dressed. He then told me to sit in the chair again, and I pleaded with him that I wanted to sleep in the bed, but he did not care. I sat in the chair after being punched in the head once again. I had a headache every day. My eyes hurt so bad because of all the crying and my head hurting. He tied my wrist up this time with rope. He pulled the rope tight. I was upset because I knew my chance of suicide was now slim to none.

This pattern of abuse went on for a little over thirty-six days. I never knew what day it was, nor did I have any concept of time. He came in and out of the room, and I kept wondering when this torture would end. The pain started to feel like little pins in my head. I had no choice but to try to adjust to what was happening around me. I wanted to end it all but had no way out.

CHAPTER 11

THE ESCAPE

One day, this creature of the night ex-boyfriend tried to tie me up with pieces of rope. My hands and wrist were so swollen from being held tightly against the corners of the chairs, and the fronts of my shoulders were so sore from being stretched in the back position that his grasp was not as secure as in the past. This monster tied my left wrist loosely on this one day. I was so tired, drained emotionally and physically from all the stress that my body had gone through that I went to move my hands, and one of the ropes loosened up. That gave me the newfound strength I needed. I was already at the bed area and could muster up enough strength in my legs, half naked, and move toward the door and window. I struggled to get out my right and left hands. The left hand was released from the grasp of the rope, and I was close enough by this time to the window. With all my strength, I used my left arm and hand to lift the chair with my right hand and threw it against the glass window. The window shattered a little. A white man outside was smoking a cigarette.

This man heard the loud noise, came over to the window and saw that I was tied to the other side of the chair. I screamed at him when I saw his face, "HELP ME!" He then went to the motel Housekeeper, who was a young Hispanic lady who appeared through the motel window at me. She disappeared quickly after seeing me.

The Housekeeper went to get the motel owner. He cut the lock on the padlock. When the door opened, I was so happy to see light enter the room. The white man who appeared taller than life now helped me get out of the bondage of the chair. The motel owner looked around the room to see if I was alone. I thanked the white man for helping to save me from the horrible ordeal ever happening again. I was grateful for him that day. The Owner and the Housekeeper were all shocked as they looked at the bruises all over my body. The bruises were all black and filled with blood; the vessels in my eyes were all blood-filled. My hands and feet were swollen, and my back bruises were ripped open. They helped me out of the chair and gave me a wet towel. I said, "Get me out, please!" I begged them not to call the cops!

The two men were able to untie my right hand. By this time, a young white girl came to the door and peeked in. She returned with a bottle of water, which I drank. She offered me a blue wrap dress with long sleeves - that was rather large - and a pair of sunglasses. I put them on to cover up. Both men were still staring at me. No one said anything else to me once I screamed and begged for them to just get me out. I asked the motel owner and the white man if they could give me some money through my dry lips. I looked out the door, and my two-seated vehicle was gone! It was nowhere to be found in that parking lot. Was it towed? I did not care to think about something so minor. My thoughts were to get out of there before my ex returned that night to the room. The white man gave me $5.00 and a ride to the nearest bus station. I took the bus to Philadelphia, where I knew I would not be found.

I arrived at 30th Street Station, broken down both mentally and physically. I did not know what to do or where to go. All I could do was try to figure a way to get back onto my feet. There was no beginning or end in sight for me. I wondered the streets of Philadelphia, nameless and hopeless. I had no identification, no idea what to do or where to go. I found what I thought was a safe place under the subway until the cops told us all who were homeless, abused, and victims, even women and children, had to leave. I just followed the crowd to wherever they were going. They led me to a shelter where I lied about my name. We had to leave in the early morning. I did not sleep all that night.

Homelessness

Shame and embarrassment controlled my thoughts every moment of the day. I could not figure out who I was. I remember being this hard-working female and living life to its fullest to now homeless, broke, and most of all, alone. I could not bring myself to even call my mother. She would hate me more than she had done before. So, I could hear her voice saying, "You made your bed, now lie in it," as she did before. Of course, there was no bed to lie in this time. However, there was pain, sorrow, and bruises that began to heal and mental torture that filled my mind. My mind played so many tricks on me at that time. I would think over and over ways of trying to commit suicide. But I also knew that I had to find some means of survival.

I found a dirty blanket and soiled food in the trash the first day and found a corner to sleep in. I just covered myself up as I had seen many homeless people and their families do time after time living on the streets. "Find the darkest corner," they would say to me, "and cover up so no one will see that you are a woman. You will be raped if they find you." I just kept moving around the city, begging for food or money to buy something to eat as the others did. I felt like I did not belong, but this was where I felt safe for the time being. Life on the street was tough, but that motel room was worse. I could live this way and be safe. I found shelter after shelter since you can only stay in them for a short time. I never gave my real name, if any name at all. I was Jane Doe to myself. I was less than a person. I had no comb to comb my hair. I wore the same dirty clothes that were torn day after day, which were now in layers so that no one knew if I was a woman or man. I smelled so bad when I came on my menstrual cycle. I would use newspaper, plastic bags, and some clothes I found on the streets as sanitary napkins. It was all horrible. I was a mess inside and out.

I begged for money; some gave pennies, nickels, and dimes; some people gave food. When days came when it would rain, I would find myself a box to curl up under, and hunger, pain, and sadness filled the small cardboard box. The seasons changed, but I did not. I learned to live on the streets and would do it until I felt I could go do something about the mess I made my entire life. My mind played tricks on me. In the shelters, some women always started fights and called me names, even without knowing me. I did nothing to them. They said I had no kids in the shelter and was taking a bed from the homeless mothers. Their words were screaming in my ears when they would tell the shelter Leader, "She doesn't belong here because she had no kids. She could sleep on the streets." As I tried to sleep, I would be hit in the head with a shoe, and even little kids were told to come over and smack me in the face as I tried hard to sleep.

I rather sleep on the streets, and that is what I did. However, I cannot remember much of what happened to me at this time in my life because I tried hard to block it out and not to ever recover it to keep my sanity. I remember one time I begged all day for money, and no one was giving me a dime. I then had to fend for myself to get food. I found a trash can with food that had been thrown out in the back of one of the restaurants. I picked through the garbage, took off the dirt or the worms on some of the food, and ate what I could until the waiter came out, saw me in the trash, and threw a bucket of water on me and the food in my hand. I looked at the waiter and said nothing. I just dropped the wet and soggy food to the ground and walked away, pushing my cart with all my found belongings. It was then that I knew I had to find a way out of this sinking hole. Time went by. A little over three years later, I walked past a store in Center City, Philadelphia.

The Turn Around - Angels are real

It was a consignment shop. At this point in my life, I cannot remember the name of the shop or the street it was on. For the most part, I blocked a lot of what had happened to me so that I could get through the rest of my life without depending on alcohol or drugs. Moving on, I saw a navy-blue suit in the window. I stared at it for a few minutes and did not notice the eyes looking back at me through the window from inside the store. An older black woman with white hair came to the door. As she did, I began to walk away. She called after me from the front door as I walked down the street, slowly pushing my cart full of stuff that was my life. I was so embarrassed and ashamed I kept walking. She called saying, "Hey lady, come here." After the third time, I turned around slowly and looked back at her with one hand on my cart. She could now see my face looking back at her. My hood covered half of my face as I hung my head low. I said nothing, just stood in silence under my soiled hat, hoodie, and big tangled hair. She motioned with her finger for me to come to her. I stood still for what seemed like an eternity. I could not move my legs. What does she want from me? I thought to myself.

After a few moments, I moved toward her, walking slowly and holding my cart with one hand and pulling it backward. I reached the door where the old gray-haired woman stood. She told me to come inside, but I slowly moved my head in the 'no' motion. I felt too dirty to be going into a store like that. It was dark from where I stood, and I feared the dark. She pulled on my long sleeve plaid jacket. I had three jackets on; it was cold that day. I cannot remember the month or year, but it was cold. I followed her inside the store. She asked if I liked the navy-blue suit in the window. I shook my head to motion, 'yes.' She said it looked like it was my size. She asked me my size. I told her that I did not know. She wanted me to try it on. I motioned with my head no. I knew that I was too dirty to be trying on clothes. I was so humiliated, embarrassed, and ashamed all at once. It was horrifying all this attention that she was giving to me. But she was nice, I thought to myself. She seemed harmless. Just a little old black woman with very white hair. She was petite and short with piercing grayish blue eyes, which I noticed the most about her up close as I had done in the window. Her eyes were like a grayish blue color, like a beautiful sunny day without smog or dirty air to pollute the skies. They were very clear.

She insisted that I try the suit on. Finally, after a few minutes, out of respect for my elders, I took the suit, not saying anything to her at all. She led me into the small dressing room on the right rear side of the store. For the first time in years, I had seen a mirror, and I looked horrible. I just stared at the person, which was me staring back. It was horrifying. My skin was light in color, much like I had lived in darkness all my life. My face, feet, and hands were dirty. They looked like someone had just thrown mud on me, and it dried up. "This is bad," I said in my mind. How did I get to this point? When? The only things that looked the same about me from what I could remember were my eyes. They were my eyes. My body, face, and hair were different, but you cannot change the eyes. They looked dark and defeated. The look of shame stared back at me for the very first time. I never tried on that suit that day.

I stood in a daze for a few moments, then snapped out of it after I heard the old woman's voice. The old woman asked, "You alright"? I said nothing. She pulled back the curtain and saw me sitting there looking at the mirror. Someone entered the store; she pulled the curtain shut. I did not want to be seen looking this way. All I could do was sit and think about if someone was taking my cart, which the old lady placed in the alley between the buildings. I looked at the navy-blue suit that was hanging on the hanger hook. I did not want to be seen or noticed in such a fine suit or clean clothes. The old woman turned her attention to the customer in the store. It was an old white lady who also had white hair, but she was 'just looking,' was what she told the black old lady with the white hair. I could hear their conversation. The customer was not in the store for anything specific nor for a long time.

The black old lady with white hair came back to check on me. I was sitting on a chair in the back of the store. I did not want her to see me looking around or think that I was stealing anything from her or her store since she left me alone. I sat with the suit in my hand and handed the clothing to her. She asked me if I was hungry. I motioned 'yes.' I was always hungry. I thought she might just be kidding me as I sat quietly. She went to the small room in the very back of the store and returned with a sandwich. It had clean wheat bread, and it was a peanut butter and jelly sandwich.

How did she know that this was my favorite sandwich? I ate it in one gulp. She watched. I had no manners when it came to eating at that time. On the streets, you had to eat your food very fast because if you did not, another homeless person who liked the food would snatch it from your hand so fast you would not see it coming if they were hungry enough. They would also punch you in the face for your food. That had happened to me plenty of times. I hunted food from trash containers behind many food places in Philadelphia for many years. It did not matter if the food was clean or dirty; if the maggots were not fully grown, it was considered good food. I never ate the mold on food; that used to freak me out. But I ate everything else; it did not matter. If I could not get money begging, then I would hunt for food.

After I ate the sandwich, I saw her staring at me with those painless greyish blue eyes. She had clear eyes which were not dull and lifeless like mine when I looked in the mirror. I just sat with my head down, trying to avoid eye contact with her. After about ten minutes, I stood up and went to move past her. She asked if she could ask me a question. I stopped in my tracks and turned around after walking a few steps passed where she stood. I pulled my head up to look at her. She asked, "What happened to you to cause you to want to live in the streets? Are you on drugs or alcohol?" I replied, "I do not remember, and no, I am not on any drug or drink any alcohol." She asked if I wanted to go to her home and sleep in a bed. I said nothing. She asked again in her quiet, calm voice. She was very calm and moved with great grace as she walked. I watched her close her store. I never answered her. She insisted that I go home with her. I do not know why this old lady would take me to her home. She did not know me.

We went out through the back door of her store. I saw that my cart was still in the alley. I was fearful that someone would take it if I went with her. She had an old Buick car, not sure what year; I don't remember that, but it was clean inside. I got into the back seat, but she wanted me to sit in the front seat. I would not dare. I was ashamed and did not want to embarrass her if anyone saw us in the car. She drove to some part of Philadelphia, not sure how long the drive was. It was in the Northeast section. She lived in one of those row homes. It was brick and nice. But I could not see much with my head down so she would not see me looking at her from the back seat. I did not make any eye contact with her. Time went on; we arrived, got out of the car, and I walked behind her into her home. It was dark; the light also seemed dim everywhere I went. I started to think. There was nothing bright about her store or home unless it was just my eyes. She asked me if I was hungry again. I motioned yes. I stood by the front door just in case she was a murderer. I thought, why was I even thinking that? I lived on the streets. I had no fear, so why fear this old lady? Anyway, I dismissed the thought because there was nothing about her that was even harmful.

Why was she trusting me? She told me to follow her to the kitchen to cook. I followed her. The kitchen light was on, and finally, some light where I could see her. She moved with grace and elegance. She had beautiful brown skin and very white hair; she was much older than I had previously thought. She only had one picture in the kitchen, and that was of a little girl, maybe her daughter or granddaughter. But I did not dare to speak. I was in this nice warm home, and I was dirty. I did not want to sit on her chair, but she insisted. She only got me to move or do anything when she insisted. She finally caught wind of that.

I sat while she cooked. The food smelled so good my stomach grew hungrier as time went by. She put the plate in front of me. It was chili and rice, and she made a simple salad. I ate it all in less than five minutes. I did not even say grace over the food as she had done. I did not stop to hear or notice anything. She just sat and ate slowly with her perfect posture. I kept my head down and ate until all the food was gone from my plate. Then I ate the salad with my fingers. She watched while still eating slowly. She asked if I wanted more, and I motioned yes. I ate everything she put in front of me. I did not know the next time I would eat clean, cooked, warm food, so I made the most of it until I was full to the brim. I drank water. I wanted nothing but water, clean water.

Now I was ready to go. I am done here. How was I going to leave? While still sitting at the table, she wanted to talk. I did not. She asked me, "Where are you from?" I replied, "I do not remember." She asked me if I have a family. I told her I did not remember. She asked how long I had been living on the streets. I told her a long time. She sensed that I did not want to give her information, and most of all, I wanted to forget, so I worked hard on forgetting. She asked me if I wanted to take a bath. I sat there thinking, yes, of course, but no, because I did not want to dirty her stuff. I was dirty, and this was where I was comfortable. I bothered no one, and no one bothered me. Now, this lady comes along and will not leave me alone. She asked me again. Then she insisted. I stood to follow her to the bathroom. She gave me a clean white towel, clean white washcloth, clean white soap, clean white socks, clean white robe, a man's sweat suit, shampoo, a comb, and a brush.

I stood in her bathroom. It was all white and very clean. It looked as if I walked out of this world and into another. I did not want to touch anything in there at all. I was dirty and smelled. There was also an oval mirror with a white wood frame around it. I was too ashamed to even look into the mirror at myself. These were the worst feelings I had while standing there. She ran the bath water and put soap for bubbles in it. The old woman with white hair left the bathroom. I sat on the toilet seat and placed the items she had given me on the floor beside me. I saw a small silver mirror sitting on the vanity across from the toilet seat. While sitting there, I saw my life flash before my eyes.

I saw my mother's face and her hate, my children being born, and my nice life, furniture, and tears filled my eyes. I cried uncontrollably, but I did so without making a sound. I did not want this lady to hear me cry. This was the first time I had cried since my first six months living on the streets. Before this time, I had no feelings. I have and can still block out my feelings. I can go someplace, be alone and disconnect myself from life and reality. I learned how to do that on the streets. I learned to be emotionless and quiet so I would not become attached to anyone or anything. Nothing matters when you live on the streets. All the emotions I had pinned down for years came back to the forefront of my mind as I sat in this clean white space. I had clean soap to wash, so why not get in the tub? So many emotions were restored. Who would have figured that? It did not matter currently. I sat there all night in my same clothes. The bubbles in the water were all now dissolved. All my emotions, shame, disgust, anger, pain, torture, and hate, were removed. I sat emotionless.

The next morning, the old woman opened the bathroom door slowly and she saw me sitting on the toilet seat and noticed that I had not gotten into the tub. She sat at my feet, looked into my eyes, and told me that she would help me get into the tub. She ran new water and sang an old church song that was familiar. "Amazing Grace How Sweet The Sound" rang out of her mouth. I watched her run the water. I had no thoughts, I just listened to how beautiful her voice was. It was clearly the voice of an Angel. She took the two hats off my head and sprayed my hair with warm water from a bottle to untangle it. She repeatedly sang the same song, "Amazing Grace How Sweet the Sound." I sat there thinking how dirty and tangled my hair was. The water was now ready. She insisted that I get into the tub and that she would finish untangling my hair.

She left the room for a moment and returned with a small stool. I was in the tub by this time. The water turned so dirty instantly under the bubbles. The water felt so good and warm. It smelled so nice; it reminded me of a valley of flowers of roses filled the air in that white bathroom. She sat down on the short round stool with silver legs at the end of the tub where my head was. She handed me the soap and washcloth. I was so embarrassed. I just busted out crying. She heard me cry and said nothing, just kept singing the Amazing Grace song. Was it the only song she knew? I told her, "Thank you for the acts of kindness and the clean water."

She had stopped singing at this time. I guess it is because I spoke. She got up to look at me face to face and resumed singing Amazing Grace again. Then she went back to her stool to finish my hair. She had a bucket she placed on that side of the tub. I washed away my tears. She finished washing my hair and began braiding it with some soft lotion-type solution. "It is manageable now," she said, then went back to singing "Amazing Grace How Sweet the Sound." I was done with the bath; she was done with my hair. She left the bathroom and returned with the navy-blue suit. Then she looked at me and started to cry. I stood still, shocked and wondering what I had done. I said nothing. She kept crying for what seemed like a very long time. She did not say any words but just cried. I stood there wishing that I could just disappear. Tears came to my eyes. I saw my grandmother in her for some reason. I missed my grandmother. This old lady is now making me remember a lot. I had to get out of here before she blamed her tears on me. I did not know how to exit her home.   I tried to move, but my legs would not move. Then she reached for my left hand and pulled me down to her level. I kneeled at her feet on both knees. She told me that Jesus loves me. I remember that my grandmother used to say that my whole childhood, and I never really knew what she meant. Now, this old lady is saying the same thing. Someone needs to tell me what this means. I don't know love. Hate was love to me my whole life. That is the love I knew. But I said nothing. I made eye contact because she was so nice and kind and wanted to see what I could do to help her stop crying. She gathered her tears in a white hanky with the little blue flowers and looked at me after drying her face.

The old white-haired lady looked into my eyes and said she had a daughter she had lost to the streets of Philadelphia years ago. That she was on drugs and died on the streets. She had run away at the age of twelve, and she never saw her again. When she saw me looking through her store window, she thought I was her under my hat and big hair behind the dirt on my face. She had hoped that she was still alive for some reason. Because I did not make real eye contact with her, she could not picture my face at all. She had lost her husband a few years ago and was alone. After she looked at my face and realized that I was not her since she could clearly see that I have a birthmark on my left cheek, she knew then, but my eyes were like her daughter's eyes, full of sadness and pain. She realized that she did not bring her daughter home but a stranger. I guess now she must realize that this is very dangerous. She had an issue with not letting go after her daughter's death. I told her that I understood death and loss.

I looked at her and again said, "Thank you." She asked if I had ever seen her daughter on the streets and showed me a picture that looked like me. It was so weird. I told her, "No, I was only living on the streets for a few years and did not know anyone. I just live among the homeless, moving from place to place." I informed her that many girls and women are on drugs and have addiction issues on the streets, but I had none of that. She asked me, "What happened to you?" I told her that I do not talk about what happened, but I am a victim of violence, which drove me to live on the streets to get away and that I never saw my ex again and do not anticipate seeing him ever in life. I told her, "Please, don't make me talk about it." The old lady left my story alone. She and I had not felt that tenderness in so long. I just hugged her back and cried small tears silently on her shoulder. She said, "You could sleep in a clean bed for one night." I replied, "Thank you for the bath, the suit, for combing my hair, the good food and clean water, and that was enough for me. I don't mind leaving and sleeping on the streets. I can always find a safe place to lay my head on the streets." I had to get out of there were my thoughts. I just wanted to get back to my cart.

The old lady fixed breakfast, and I ate fast as usual. She said nothing to me until it was time for us to leave. The old lady gave me a $5.00 bill and told me, "Take care, and may God create new beginnings in your life." Those were her exact words. We got back into her car, and she drove to her store as I sat in the back seat. I told her to let me off anywhere. I had my layers of clothing in a bag now and was wearing the navy-blue suit and some raggedy old sneakers. She drove her car to the same parking spot behind her store. I got out, grabbed my cart, and went on my way. I had five dollars in my pocket, so that was enough for me to eat and live a little while longer.

That morning, I looked into the trash and saw the Philadelphia Enquirer Newspaper advertising new casinos in Atlantic City, New Jersey. It caught my attention; I opened it and saw that there was a job fair that day. I left my cart in another alley. I used my five dollars to catch the train to Atlantic City. When I arrived at the train station on the Atlantic City end, I went into the bathroom. The old lady had given me a comb, and I combed my hair again. Happy that I had a comb, it was now in a neat ponytail, as neat as I could make it. I stood in the long line at the job fair and waited my turn.

The Interview

Finally, it was my turn. I was so excited and very nervous. It was my first time trying to get a job in over three years, and I had no confidence in myself. But the clean water washed some of the shame off me. I was somewhat ready for this next chapter of my life. I had on clean clothes. It was not the best interview attire, but this is all that I had that was remotely presentable. I had low self-esteem my whole life, and my mother taught us how to act happy and loving, so I had acting skills from day one and learned from the best.

I filled out the application at the table as I waited for the interviewer to sit at my table. It was a mixed woman. I remember her name to this day. She was very nice. She oversaw the Housekeeping Department at the Showboat Casino. She asked me my name and told me to tell her a little about myself. I was stuck at that moment in time because my last few years were horrible, and I had nothing to tell her. It had just dawned on me that I had no story to tell her about myself that was positive. I sat quietly, and tears began to fill my eyes. She noticed. The interviewer asked if I was ok. She got up to get me a tissue, and the people next to our table noticed. She sat back down. I told her that I did not have a positive life and there was no good story about me that I could tell, which I did not realize until she asked me the question. However, I began to beg her for a job. She asked, "What kind of work did you do in the past?"

I replied, "The banking industry, and I can type, but I'm willing to do anything to get the job. I needed money to get my life together." She asked me why. I began telling her my story. She was shocked at my story and asked, "Where is your ex-boyfriend now?" I replied, "I do not know. I never saw him again after escaping from the motel room that day." She looked at me, and tears started to form in her eyes. I told her how I got money from an old black lady with white hair and greyish piercing blue eyes to get there to the interview; she inspired me to want to get off the streets. This interviewer told me she had an opening as a housekeeper and offered me the job. But I had no identification and would have to get that somehow. She gave me the number to Catholic Charities in Atlantic City. They helped me to get identification for the job.

I started working at the Casino, worked a lot of hours, and finally found a place to live in a rooming home that the Charities people set up for me. I worked two jobs, went to school, and concentrated on reviving my life. I stayed in hibernation and kept to myself. I was very leery about dating anyone or being on the streets. I did not want to run into my ex any place. A lot of places I went to only brought bad memories for me. I had a job, and I blocked them all out. I found out later that my ex had passed away from being sick with some sort of stomach problem, and then I knew it was all behind me. I would never see him again. I felt free from him now.

CHAPTER 12

STARTING OVER

This point of my life was so difficult. Starting over is all I ever tried and wanted to do. I wanted the new beginnings that the old lady had mentioned to me months before this day. But I blocked out everything about my life. I was ok with myself. I finally worked hard enough to get an apartment and started getting furniture. I met a nice guy from Pittsburg and was happy with him. He treated me nicely, and I was in love with him. We stayed together for years until he decided to cheat around on me with a girl on his job; I caught him with her. I broke up with him and never looked back. I developed more meaningful friendships over the years while working hard, two and three jobs at a time.

Then I was determined to start moving back to developing a relationship with my mother since I heard she was getting sick. I visited her in the hospital and at her home, did her hair, and tried my hardest to get her to love me. My life went on like that until the day she died. She never showed any love toward me or any kind word. Each time she saw me, her words were negative for me, "You are fat, you are ugly, your hair does not look right," time and time again. I hated to go around her, but that was my mother, so I had to. I spent a lot of time over the years around my grandmother and grandfather. They loved me, and I loved them more than anyone else in my life. They were always there for me up to the day they died. I could talk to my grandmother about anything. Even with Alzheimer's, when my siblings and I cared for my grandparents as they aged up to the day they died, they both were still enjoyable. They still showed love toward me, and that was all that really mattered.

Although my life at that point had taken a turn for the better, things were still a struggle for me to this day. My struggles include family, there are siblings to this day that do not want anything to do with me, and there are men from my past that I see now that I wish I had never ever had sex with or even associated with. All those different boys and men I gave my body to were useless. I was useful to them, and that was the extent of every one of my relationships. Although young, I thought that I could find love this way. I cannot remember all of those boys I had sex with as a teen; some names I can recall, most I cannot recall. But they remember me. The rumors from the past still haunt me today when I am seen in my old neighborhood at funerals and family gatherings. But to no avail, I don't care. My heart has no one feeling of love or hate for any of these people who do not see the change in my life. Most do not even know this story. They can just read this book. Some who read my story will be upset, which does not matter to me. The sole reason for my troubles is that I tried to be a people pleaser my whole life. Those days were over in 2002 when my mother passed away.

Years passed and I decided that other people's problems in my family were not my problem. I have provided for so many, and the only people who have been there for me consistently are my youngest brother and youngest sister. I am not saying that my siblings never helped, but after my mother passed, things changed just as they do in many families today. The disappointment of it all is that I failed to build relationships over the years. Relationship building is not an easy task for anyone. It involves trust, love, commitment, dedication, honesty, and many other factors. In the past, I have never seen any positive relationships with my mother and her male friends or partners. She had awesome relationships with those around her who loved her, but with her children, things were different. My siblings all have a story to tell regarding her and their relationships with her, some good and some bad. My goal or deed before I leave this earth is to have an impact on the younger generation. I have learned so many things that need to be passed on to prevent today's young ladies and girls from going through negative energy and behaviors such as abuse or any negative act from anyone.

Stay away from people who will not help you grow positively; I do not care who they are. Our hearts and minds are always to be protected, especially the body. We must teach young ladies that our body is our temple, and what we do to it speaks to it mentally and places it in our hearts; it all has a lasting effect.

Once I got on my feet and recovered most things that I had lost, I returned to find the old lady with the white hair and greyish piercing blue eyes on the street stores of Philadelphia, but she was no longer there. To my Angel, wherever you may be, thank you for watching over me and helping me through the door of opportunity with $5.00, a hug, and a tear. Thank you for the song you sang over and over until it radiated in my mind every day. Amazing Grace is such a sweet sound. I did not realize then that the universe had sent me an Angel to carry me along. In one 24-hour period of my life, it was saved, and I was set free. Thank you.

Young people, please know that pain is only a 4-letter word and can impact your life in two ways. One is a lesson, and the second is a test. Both can be hurtful and drive you into deeper thoughts of negative vibrations and attract negative people, places, and things. The lessons may hurt, but we must learn to turn our thoughts into gratitude to begin the healing process. I forgive everyone from the beginning of my birth who has had a lesson of pain in their grips for me. I forgive my siblings, cousins, and everyone who has spoken negative words, curses, and vibrations that were not for my higher good. I forgive most importantly myself for my responsibility in any action against anyone and wish for forgiveness from those who I hurt over the years due to my hate, torture, and violent beginnings.

Starting over is never easy. But at least you recognize that. Once you at least begin to move forward in the act of starting over, find spirituality to help you along the way. My Lord and Savior Christ Jesus saved me from myself and forgave me for everything I have ever done. I had to learn through other spiritual teachings to break free from the shackles of my mind, break free from the sexual bondages from my partners of times past and present. Use affirmations that will help you to stay motivated with positive energy. Learning to produce good seeds, we must learn to plant in good soil. Healthy living should be our goal, and spirituality should be our focus. I found that in my pain that inspirations come from hitting rock bottom. Today, when I feel lost, alone or hopeless, I listen to my heart and move forward honestly. It is still hard for me to empathize with people who don't have to struggle. I think the people who struggle are heroic because they don't give up.

CHAPTER 13

THE LESSON- DATING & RELATIONSHIPS

Words of wisdom from me to you when dating, please pay attention to the signs. Don't shell out money to him or for him while dating; never loan him money. Please be sure that he is responsible for his child support. If he cannot support his own children, love them or respect the mother, you may want to pass on him. There is someone out there who is of sound mind who can express selfless acts of love and affection toward you. Never go with a guy who stalks you while dating or provide a place for him to live. He should have a place of his own which will show that he has a sense of purpose, pay bills, show responsibility, a stable ground and job. Please do not be his security blanket in this game called life. He is to provide security and protection for you, not vice versa. I had to learn that in marriage. Lesson learned, I ignored the red flags.

True, purposeful, and meaningful relationships will not be painful. We all process pain in different ways. I was not good at processing mine, as you can read. I slept in an actual graveyard after my mother died for three days. It was a cold November evening, and only a few years ago after reading a text that said, "That is why your husband left you and your children died, you will die alone" from someone you love so much, a sibling. Why mention something in a text? First of all, cowards do that. Secondly, that person does not even know what they are talking about. Just because that person has children living and has not experienced what I have in the way that I have proves that they don't really know me. So, this story is a lesson for them, a reflection as well. Karma comes back, so watch the spells you sow onto someone from your heart; let this be a lesson for you all as well. Sow kindness at all times, and show gratitude.

The reason for sleeping in the dark, cold, and quiet place on the ground is because I wanted to be there at her grave site to tell her that I am sorry to have been such a disappointment, and my son is buried over her grave. I slept at the foot of my mother's and my son's ashes. Thinking of death while alive in such a way made me realize that I am not as healed as I thought. Not as strong as I thought I was and had endured so much. But the reality is that PAIN is real in my life today. After the third day of sleeping and spending the long cold days there, it was no change. No one looked for me. I turned off my phone because I did not want to wake up and realize that I had yet made another mistake.

I could have died of hypothermia. Why I did not die on those cold and lonely nights, I do not know. But my lesson from that experience is that I have to live on purpose. Nothing more or less. I no longer have to ask myself, why am I here? What is my purpose? I know why and what. To write this book to help others and to leave a legacy for girls, women, and teens to know that you can do it. You can survive all sorts of circumstances in your life as long as you stay of sound mind. It was hard to recall a lot of my story due to different types of therapy over the years, and hypnotic therapy was the most successful which was needed. The pain was relevant and real. The thoughts of suicide were real at that time. I can function with depression, as an alcoholic can function through their work life. In hiding, behind closed doors, crying in the dark. Today, I cannot say that my life is the most rewarding life that I have lived thus far. By far, it is not. But the lessons I learned along the way are forgiveness, and that thoughts of positive thinking are a way of life, which is a choice we should make. It is not easy to be reprogrammed, especially when the circumstances are what they are when you look at your life. Why not look at those things in another way? Every night and morning, just say what you are thankful for today. My list is endless daily. Listen to morning prayers; they help.

I am thankful for my home office and being able to finally put these words on paper, thankful for hot and cold water when I shower or bathe daily, thankful for the food and the round belly sitting before me, thankful that I can use my fingers, toes, and so much more. Please make an effort to build confidence within yourself. There are plenty of YouTube videos that will help; I seek them daily. Yes, it is difficult to switch gears and build self-confidence; no good thing in life is easy. I am living proof. Find peace and confidence within yourself; you don't need a partner for that—just a spiritual awakening. Seek spirituality, whatever your heart is leading you to. Mine changed because "Jesus loves you and so do I," and the amazing grace that will fill your life will become the sweet sound that you will hear daily in your heart of gratitude. I promise you that you will see change in your life.

Marriage is another chapter in my life, which I will present another book to you later. I will share the experiences that taught me a whole new level of lessons. My lesson in my marriage is that I saw signs that I ignored. I do not ignore them today. I also learned not to tell my story to someone unless they truly care enough to protect me from the threat of living on the streets again. Not to allow a man to come and live with me if he cannot hold up his end of responsibility in his own home. If he treats his mother better than he treats his wife, that is a sign as well. Same gifts at Christmas and birthdays, infidelity, theft, and dishonesty are all huge red flags. Love does not hurt at all. I hurt a lot in marriage, trying to learn how to love from someone who did not know how. That was my fault; I should not have married, and that is my regret. Most importantly, he must know how to love, act on love, be emotionally sound, no yelling, and be lovingly warm enough to tell when something is wrong and at least attempt to actively fix it. Those things were important to me, and those lessons I learned. I have my first marriage to thank for those lessons. Marriage may not be for everyone. Maybe it is not for me. I am fine with that. I may just live with my next partner in peace and harmony. I know many couples who live together for years in a more peaceful existence than those who are married.

Thank you for reading my book and sharing my story with others. This book was not intended to offend or hurt anyone in any way. I am just telling my story and how I felt and still feel about issues then and now. I look back over my life and can now see the purpose of it all. Since the first book - this is version two - I toned down some of the traumatic sections so that teens, young and old, can read it. I have a lot of people in my family who do not like my story, and old flames as well, which all of them are totally irrelevant. They do not even have the compassion to say that they are sorry that I lost their children, not one of those fathers, but they will have to pay for that on their death beds, I will not be there. Those who did not want to be mentioned played a crucial part in my life's lessons to get me here. I am ok with the talk behind my back. I forgave them all a long time ago. The bondages are broken anyway. I have no ties; those who are your family are irrelevant to who God has your tribe to be. Tribes for me are much better than most of my family. If your family loves you truly, they will seek you out and stay in touch. I am forgotten by most. It is all good. God has work for me to do with helping others.

To write books like this is my passion for learning that your pain is something that you can share. If your life seems negative and painful, write it out and make a stand to help others to overcome or prevent them from taking the wrong turn and making wrong decisions. Know that our choices in life can affect the rest of our lives.

Today, I have no children, more meaningful relationships with a small select group of my friends who are part of my tribe, and no true relationship with my siblings, nieces, or nephews. I had no relationship with the man who I thought was my real father up until 2008 after seeing my birth certificate. I sometimes feel alone, but I have friends who I can call who are there for me, and I am grateful for that. Singleness is a choice for me now. I know that I will have true love because it will be if it is intentional. When that time comes, it will have been well worth the wait. My spiritual journey is full of patience and control. I will embrace my next meaningful partner and be free to love unconditionally for the first time in my life. My life as it sits now today is just lovely. I am FREE!

I look forward to writing that book too.

PAIN is just a 4-letter word in our lives. We can experience pain in several different ways, mind, and body. However, I have learned through my journey in this lifetime that PAIN is just that. It can be healed, it can be forgiven, and it can be used to help someone else to heal. That is the purpose of my PAIN. I am convinced now that it is just a 4-letter word meant to help someone else. This four-letter word was meant to help me heal all the forces set out to break me, to distract me from the true purpose of my life. The Most High has turned my PAIN into purpose. That is why so many other girls and I cry in the dark. The PAIN is real. The things that we go through are real but not meant to drive us into the pits of hell on earth. I truly believe that our choices at times can cause us pain. It did that for me.

I forgive myself first, then I forgive and have forgiven others. I must forgive daily to heal the pain I may be feeling. I look at PAIN differently now. Purpose is what drives me positively, and love does the rest. I had and continue to start each day with positive affirmations knowing that I matter in this lifetime. Love yourself, forgive yourself and others, and then allow the pain to help you grow on purpose. You will then be able to say that your life is now fulfilled, complete, and pain-free.

Made in the USA
Las Vegas, NV
19 November 2022